KARCH KIRALY'S CHAMPIONSHIP VOLLEYBALL

JON HASTINGS, editor

A Fireside Book

Published by Simon & Schuster

New York · London · Toronto · Sydney · Tokyo · Singapore

FIRESIDE
Rockefeller Center
1230 Avenue of the Americas
New York, New York 10020

FIRESIDE and colophon are registered trademarks
of Simon & Schuster Inc.

Manufactured in the United States of America

10 9 8 7 6 5 4 3 2 1

Library of Congress Cataloging-in-Publication Data

Kiraly, Karch.
    [Championship volleyball]
    Karch Kiraly's championship volleyball / Karch Kiraly; Jon
Hastings, editor.
        p. cm.
    "A Fireside book."
    1. Volleyball. I. Hastings, Jon. II. Title. III. Title:
Championship volleyball.
    GV1015.3.K55 1990
    796.325—dc20   90-34595
                                                          CIP

ISBN 0-684-81466-8

Photos of Steve Timmons on page 61 and Eric Sato on page 72 courtesy of Joshua Lee.
Photo of "Russian leaper" on page 133 courtesy of Colin Crawford.
Instructional photos of Karch Kiraly on pages 18, 19, 20, 21, 22, 28, 38, 39, 52, 63, 64,
  68, 69, are by Dennis Steers.
Photos of Karch Kiraly on pages 27, 35, 47, 67, 93, 145 World Copyright © All-Sport
  USA.
Photos on pages 15, 111, 137 World Copyright © All-Sport USA/Bruce Hazelton.
Photo on page 77 World Copyright © All-Sport USA/Photo by Mike Powell.
Photo on page 125 World Copyright © All-Sport USA/Rick Stewart.
Photo on page 171 World Copyright © All-Sport USA/Steve Dunn.
Photo on page 57 Copyright © Bruce Hazelton.
Photo on page 117 Copyright © Dave Middlecamp.
Illustrations by Mary Sarah Quinn.

I'd like to dedicate this book to William Morgan, who in 1895 invented the game of volleyball—a sport that has afforded me so many thrilling opportunities and wonderful memories for the last twenty-eight years.

ACKNOWLEDGMENTS

There are a lot of people I need to thank for making this book possible. Volleyball is first and solely a team sport, and without my teammates and coaches over the years I would never have had the opportunity to play on the best team in the world, or to experience the excitement of winning a Triple Crown (Olympic Games, World Cup, and World Championship in succession) or any other championship for that matter. Thank you very, very much, everyone.

Thanks, Bruce Anderson, for helping to teach me what it takes to communicate my ideas clearly. Thank you very much, Tim Rafael, for helping me get all of my ideas across—across the ocean, that is, with all of your time and patience on the fax. And thank you, John Diemer, for helping break the ground to make projects like this possible.

Special thanks to my family for supporting me, wherever I happen to be; special thanks to Jerry Solomon and Lon Monk for believing in us; special thanks to Lorene Graves and Elena Doyle for all of your time and energy; special thanks to Jon Hastings for your soft editing touch; and, lastly but mostly, special thanks to my wife, Janna, for helping me put it all in perspective, and for everything else.

CONTENTS

FOREWORD

When I first met Karch Kiraly in the late spring of 1978, he was a lean high school senior with a reputation that already extended up and down the California coast.

We were opponents in the Marine Open beach tournament in Manhattan Beach, California—an event I had no business playing in. The precocious Karch, on the other hand, was already right in his element.

It was my misfortune to draw Karch in the tournament's opening round. Despite the fact that my partner Andy Schroeder and I were both four years older (and presumably more experienced) than our primary adversary, we were the ones nervously warming up in the presence of this volleyball "phenom."

It should not surprise anyone familiar with Karch's volleyball talents that he and his partner Jon Lee quickly turned the match into a rout. It was 4–0 before I managed our first sideout on a feeble "cut shot" that landed just inside the ropes.

Karch, sensing my nervousness, complimented me on the shot. The compliment was not condescending, but rather very sincere. Karch and his partner then graciously finished off the rout. It probably wasn't one of the most memorable triumphs for the most famous volleyball player in the history of the sport, but it is still fresh in my mind.

I mention this first encounter only because, after countless dealings with Karch since becoming the editor/publisher of *Volleyball Monthly* magazine, I have not seen him lose his gentleman's approach to volleyball—a sport that he has helped elevate in status all over the world. It's not so much the two Olympic gold medals, two beach volleyball world championships, four All-American awards while at UCLA, two Pan American Games gold medals, a World Cup title, etc., that have made Karch Kiraly so infinitely popular in the worldwide volleyball community— it's the manner in which he has accomplished these incredible feats.

There have been players who could jump as high as the forty inches Karch soars. There have been players who could cover the court with the catlike quickness that has become a Kiraly trademark. There even have been some players who have competed with the same desire as Karch. But there hasn't been—ever— another player who has put all of those great qualities together in one versatile package, or who has dedicated himself so totally to the sport, both on and off the court. That's what has helped make Karch Kiraly stand out during his fifteen-year career. Long after his playing days are over, the Karch Kiraly legacy will thrive.

Karch's book is his latest contribution to the sport of volleyball. Filled with the insight and knowledge you would expect from the best player in the world, this book is must reading for beginners and advanced players alike.

I'm thankful for the opportunity to work with him on this book—and finally to repay that early compliment. Nice shot, Karch!

—Jon Hastings
San Luis Obispo, California
January 1990

INTRODUCTION

Over 30 million people played volleyball in the United States last year. Some played a rudimentary game, having fun without worrying about complicated offenses, backrow attacks, or double-stack blocking schemes. Others were honing their skills in recreational leagues or on school teams, looking for new wrinkles to add to their teams' offensive and defensive systems.

All of us (myself included) could have benefited from a refresher course in individual skills and team play. That's what this book is all about. It's aimed at helping all volleyball players improve—whether their goal is winning in their Sunday-night league, or at the Olympic games.

If you are a recreational player, you can use the basic instructions and drills in the early chapters of this book to fine-tune your bumping, setting, digging, serving, and spiking techniques. After all, there's plenty of room for improvement in everyone's game. And I hope you'll also be intrigued enough by some of the more advanced team material that I present later on in the book to want to try it out yourselves. To me, improving your whole team's level of play is one of the most rewarding things in volleyball—and that part of the book gives you and your friends plenty of basic team concepts, drills, and plays to work at.

More experienced players should find plenty of material they can use in the advanced team play chapters. I've included some of my most memorable volleyball experiences, as well as a few anecdotes about my teammates on the US national team, and about playing in the '84 and '88 Olympics. The book probably won't answer all of your questions about those teams or about how we won two gold medals, but I do cover a lot of the techniques, strategies, and training that we used to get there—I'm sure that it will come in handy in turning your team's play into a more sophisticated, more potent attack.

With luck, I'll get to tell you more about those national teams at some other time—but by then who knows which team will be best—which team will have the new secrets that the rest of the world will hunger for?

People ask me if I'm a writer. I say, "No, but I write." For me, writing is a lot harder than volleyball. I can tell you that I've been working very hard at something besides athletic preparation for the last few years. It's been a tremendous learning experience for me to try to describe in words what comes so naturally on the court. The old saying is true: "The best way to learn something is to teach it."

For these reasons, I'm very glad for the opportunity to write this book. I guess you could call it my way of trying to perpetuate the sport's tradition of excellence—that often inspired me and even compelled me to spend those extra hours sweating inside the gym or out on the beach.

If this book helps just one player improve his or her game, or one coach teach volleyball a little more successfully, then I'll feel like the task has been worth the effort. So good luck to all of you—I'm rooting for you.

KARCH KIRALY'S

CHAMPIONSHIP

VOLLEYBALL

1

THE BUMP

I'd like to get started by talking about my background as a volleyball player and how I was able to build a foundation of skills starting with that cornerstone of every player's game, the forearm pass, or, as we call it, the bump. Anyone aspiring to be a solid volleyball player absolutely must master the art of the bump. The bump is so important that we'll cover it first, even though the serve initiates play in an actual game.

Passing is the most critical skill for the success of any volleyball team. You may have six players on the floor who are able to defy gravity with their jumping ability (like the Cuban team) and are strong enough to make the gym floor bend with their crushing spikes (like the Soviet team), but all of their ability is worthless unless at least two of them are also expert passers. The top setters in the world can't chase down passes headed for the cheap seats, but even mediocre setters can be successful if their passes are reliable. I can't stress enough the importance of learning how to control the ball with the forearm pass. It's the foundation of any strong volleyball team, both indoors and out.

Good passing simply means good ball control. Volleyball

offenses differ, so top passers can't just practice getting the ball to the same spot every time, but instead must be able to pass the ball to the spot the setter calls for.

In the Beginning, There Was the Bump

My father, Las, escaped from Hungary in 1956, during the revolt against the Soviet-backed regime. He grew up playing soccer and volleyball in school, and had been a member of the Hungarian national junior volleyball team. So naturally I was nurtured on the two sports in which he had some experience. People in the United States find it hard to believe that I never played organized basketball or football, and that I only played a little baseball.

Las and my mom, Toni, brought me to Santa Barbara, California, during his internship year of medical school. That was the summer of 1967, when I was six years old. This was our first exposure to a year-round temperate climate. Of course, my dad had to take advantage of this by playing volleyball at the beach during what little free time he had. On the weekends, he'd bring me along. That was my earliest exposure to volleyball.

I'm lucky to have such patient and understanding parents. Some parents push athletics on their children at the expense of their schoolwork, even if the kids aren't enthusiastic about the sport. My mom says my dad forced me to play at first, although I don't remember it that way. The important thing is that I remember a lot of encouragement and support from both of them—I played only if I wanted to. That's why even after all the years I've played, I rarely get bored with the game.

My dad and I started by playing a simple game. We counted how many times we could bump the ball back and forth. At first it seemed impossible to make ten bumps in a row; that alone took over a few months to master. That was the only game I could play for the first two years. I was too small to learn to spike, and my hands were too small to set the ball overhand. It's hard to believe what tremendous things have come from such a humble beginning, but that early training in ball control is the reason I fell in love with the sport. That simple game shows me how important solid basics are in any sport—without mastering that game I could never have played volleyball at higher levels. We still have some home movies of us playing that game buried somewhere in my parents' garage. In those movies, I was so small, the ball looks like it could have knocked me over. One day I hope to show my children those movies. They'll get a good laugh when they see how I looked when I was learning.

When I was nine, my dad and 2 other guys let me play on a court for the first time. That was a huge step up—I actually got to try what I'd been watching other people do for three years. The experience lit a fire in me that's still raging today. That fire is a desire to be better every time I step onto a volleyball court, indoors or out. I said my dad and 2 others, not 10, because in beach volleyball only 2 play on a side, even though the net is the same height and the court is the same size. The best part of playing beach doubles is that, to be successful, a player can't have any glaring weakness in his game. But I'll talk about that in the chapter on beach volleyball.

After that we moved back to Michigan for three years so that my dad could finish medical school. He resumed playing indoors at club tournaments throughout the state, which meant long drives through horrendous weather. Despite that, I tagged along whenever he let me. I'd spend a few minutes bumping the ball with him when he wasn't exhausted from playing. The rest of the time I just watched or bumped the ball against a wall in the corner. It doesn't sound like much fun, but it was better than freezing outside in the snow.

There's one other autobiographical detail that I should mention. When I was eight years old, I was playing in the backyard with some of my friends, doing cartwheels. I reached for the ground with my left arm, but found a foot-deep hole instead. I dislocated my elbow. Ironically, my parents were at the 1968 Olympics in Mexico City watching the Americans beat the Soviet volleyball team in a monumental upset. Even now, the elbow bends about 10 degrees backward whenever I extend it. What had been my worst accident as a kid has become a boon to me as an adult. The extra flexibility in my elbow lets me keep both arms fully extended when I pass a volleyball.

The Rules of Good Bumping

This brings me to the first rule of great bumping: keep your forearms locked together as tightly as you can to establish a larger and, just as important, a flatter surface off which you can volley the ball.

The second key is the grip you choose to hold your hands together so you can lock your elbows. When my dad first taught me, he showed me how to use the position in figure 1, where you

Figure 1. My first grip: hold the flat of one hand with the other and place your thumbs side by side.

grab the flat of one hand with your other hand and place your thumbs side by side. When I was in the ninth grade my junior high school coach, Bob Moore, taught me the fist method shown in figure 2; for this grip you wrap one hand around the other fist,

Figure 2. The "fist" grip: wrap one hand around the other (held in a fist) and place your thumbs side by side.

again putting the thumbs side by side. Neither of these seemed to work well enough: the first method didn't let me turn my forearms outward enough for a flat platform, and the second method let my hands slip apart so that my two forearms were not balanced.

My style has evolved to where I now use three different grips for three different tasks. The first, shown in figure 3, is for serve

Figure 3. **Try this grip for receiving serves. Put your left hand between your right index and middle fingers, then bring your thumbs side by side.**

reception. I actually put my left hand between my right index and middle fingers, then put both thumbs together. This grip is flexible enough to allow me to form a flat surface in any position. When you are passing serves that don't spin, the path of the ball is unpredictable and you often have to pass the ball from outside your centerline.

The second grip, shown in figure 4, is for passing free balls (when an opponent sends a weak and high shot back over the net). That's where I interlace all of my fingers and keep them straight. Free-ball passes require even more than the usual precision: free balls are so easy to control that your teammates expect nothing less than a perfect pass.

Figure 4. Try using this grip for passing free balls. Interlace your fingers, with your palms facing each other and your thumbs together.

The final grip, shown in figure 5, is really not a grip at all, but more like the last thread that barely holds your arms together. This is for defense, when your arms need to move individually because you have so little time to react on hard-driven spikes.

You should find a suitable grip with which you feel comfortable, because there's no one correct technique. Lock the meaty bottom part of your palms (underneath your little finger) together, and keep your forearms as flat as possible. Your back, as shown in figure 6, should be perpendicular to the floor, and your knees should be bent when you are first learning (later, when you've become an expert, your legs might end up in different positions when you're tracking down difficult serves). Your body

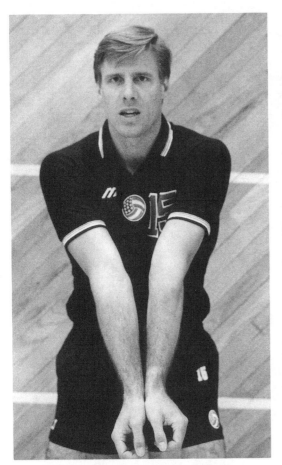

Figure 5. I position my arms and hands like this on defense. Keep your hands "unlinked" so that you can pass balls on either side of your body.

Figure 6. Here's a side view of how to position yourself to get ready to pass the ball.

will move up as a whole to meet the ball, with the arms and the back rising, and the knees straightening.

What type of footwork should you use? The primary goal of moving your feet is to get your body within arm's distance of the ball. Try to shuffle your feet back and forth. You should avoid crossing your legs. Using cross-legged footwork will leave you tangled up like a pretzel if the approaching ball changes directions. If you can, center yourself on the ball. Unfortunately, 95 percent of the serves you'll see will move erratically because they have no spin, so you'll rarely receive serves in your centerline. It takes years of practice, but you can learn to be just as comfortable passing the ball from your left or right side when you can't meet it straight down your centerline.

Now that you have mastered the arm and body position and the hand grip, where should you pass the ball? The ideal location is just slightly right of the center of the court. The perfect pass lands about 12 feet from the right sideline and only 1 or 2 feet away from the net. It should be close to the net because that's the position from which the setter can best run the offense. On the USA team we actually tried to make the pass land right on top of the tape, allowing the setter to jumpset every time, touching the ball eight or nine feet above the ground.

Passing requires intangible skills, too. One of the most important elements of great serve reception is concentration. You can't ever take your eyes off the ball, no matter what drill you're in. The easiest way to make yourself do this is to attempt to look "through" the ball. Don't look at the seams of the ball or at the valve. I find it's easier to pretend that I'm seeing right through to the backside. When your opponent steps up to serve, never look at him; look instead directly through the ball, and lock your focus onto it a few seconds before he actually starts serving. That way your concentration is locked on. It also helps you get into the flow of the ball, almost feeling where its path will lead. The ball sometimes seems to move in slow motion when I am concentrating really well.

Sometimes your opponents will try to intimidate you by staring at you before they serve. You can avoid the cold-war tactics by staring at the ball instead of their eyes. It tells the server, "Hey, I'm ready for anything you've got—give it to me." To some extent, conditioning is also a key element in concentration, so it's important to be in good shape and stay focused.

This brings up the next aspect of serve reception—confidence. With practice on easy serves, a player develops confidence. This leads into a never-ending cycle: the better you become, the more confidence you build, the more your coach can challenge you, and with success, you build even more confidence. To handle any serve that your opponents can muster, you've got to know beforehand that you will receive it perfectly. With a free ball, you know that you will control it easily. Just transfer that attitude over to when more difficult serves come at

you. Find a grip you're comfortable with and practice a lot—
you'll soon feel you can handle the most lethal jump-serve.

Drills

Athletes practice specific skills, in volleyball or any sport, so that
we can repeat the practiced actions precisely when they're called
for in competition. We practice them over and over so that we're
positive we'll do them correctly when we need to.

Here's a drill that will help you learn one of the absolute
basics: how to pass from any angle. Standing with your right
shoulder toward a wall, bump the ball against the wall sideways.
If you can hit the same brick or board on the wall from anywhere
up to a distance of about six or seven yards away, that's excellent
control. Do sets of 10 or 20 toward a particular spot. Then turn
around and repeat from the left side. You should be able to accurately bump the ball to your left and right.

Then stand facing into a corner and alternate hitting targeted
spots on each of the two walls. Take the ball in your centerline
but then guide it to the left wall, then to the right wall, left, right,
in sets of 10 repetitions increasing to 30.

In the two-passer system (which I'll explain later) popularized by the US men's team, Bob Ctvrtlik and I often received
balls at odd angles because we had to cover the whole court.
Top-flight volleyball players distinguish themselves by how they
can adjust to novel plays as each rally unfolds. Coaches have to
teach their players not only how to center themselves on the ball
when passing, but also how to pass perfectly when (as in most
cases) they can't reach that centered position. Be prepared for the
unexpected by practicing the unexpected.

Here's a drill that teaches players to begin passing consistently in live situations. Three players are needed: a server, a
passer (standing in the left or the right half of the court), and a
target player (standing at the net) who judges whether each pass
is perfect or not.

The server competes with the passer and the object is to win
three points in a row. If the server forces the passer into making
three bad passes in a row, then the server wins and becomes the
target. If the passer makes three perfect passes in a row, he wins

and becomes the target. The loser always stays in the same spot. Service errors count for the passer.

As you might guess, the passer has the advantage because it's so difficult for the server to force three mistakes in a row. So try not to get stuck at the serving spot—you could be there all day while the other two guys keep counting up all of their victories.

We normally played for about 5 to 10 minutes with each player counting up the total number of points. The player with the fewest points does the most push-ups and vice versa. About halfway through the drill you can have the passer switch halves of the court so everybody plays on each side with equal time.

The fun part of the drill is what criteria the third player uses to judge whether the passes are perfect. Often the pass is not considered acceptable unless it's within 3 feet of the net and about 12 feet from the right sideline. The other fun part is when one player has two points in a row and is on the verge of winning the game, because this puts a lot of pressure on the other player and simulates competitive conditions.

"Passing Frenzy" is the best purely repetitive drill. Get a bucket of balls, a feeder, a server, a passer, and a target. The server stands at the back line and serves balls, one after the other, as fast as the feeder can give them to him. The object is not to ace the passer every time, but to make the passer work in rapid fire, about a ball per second. At first the passer feels awkward not being able to watch the pass go to the net (you have to look up for the next serve); instead, he or she must concentrate on getting into a passing "groove." After the bucket runs out, the players rotate. Once everyone has passed from the left side of the court, repeat the drill on the right side.

Here's a drill that forces you to practice all of the things I've discussed. Aldis Berzins (a star member of the US team from 1977 to 1985) and I had to do it many times a few years back to improve our serve reception under pressure. At the end of practice, all of our players except Aldis and me went to the far end of the gym, where they served at us as hard as they possibly could. Most of the players would stand at least 30 feet behind the endline, so that the serves would drift around more while traveling the longer distance. We had to receive 20 serves in a row perfectly (serving errors counted for us), and the entire team could not leave practice until we succeeded. This simulated competition levels of intensity and pressure. Once we got up to about 12 perfect passes, our nerves started to tighten and it was as though we were passing in the fifth game with the score 15–15 against the Soviets. There was added pressure because although our teammates were supportive, they didn't want to spend the night in the gym if we couldn't finish. It once took us an hour and a half to finish. Considering the fact that the serves are as tough as possible, coaches might like to start with a more reasonable number, like 5 or 10 serves instead of 20.

The most common problem players encounter when trying to master serve reception is one of direction—the ball won't go where it is supposed to. There could be several reasons for this. Maybe you aren't holding your arms tightly together and so they don't form one flat surface. You might not be centering yourself—taking the ball on your midline. Or you may be swinging your arms too hard instead of using both arms and your legs to guide the ball to the proper spot.

To correct the problem, imagine that there is a string, or an arc, between you and the target—just try to make the ball follow that path. Get a partner, stand on a line about 20 feet apart, and make the ball go along the line, back and forth. Keep your arms straight and flat, center yourself, and use your legs. It'll come.

Understand the basics now? Because serve reception is really a very basic skill, yet it is also the most important: without a good pass, no team can be successful. Period. You get your arms, hands, feet, legs, and eyes ready, then you get your mind ready—physical and mental preparation put you well on your way to becoming a great passer.

2

SETTING

The setter is the most important player on the court. He has to be the smartest player—mastering, developing, and adjusting his coach's game plan throughout a match. It's the most difficult job in volleyball, but also one of the most rewarding, since the setter plays such a critical role on every team.

To me, touching a volleyball overhand, whether passing or setting, is the most elegant skill in the sport. Setting is really a massaging of the ball, a gentle touch among the more animal, powerful techniques such as hitting and blocking. For that reason, overhand setting is probably the most difficult skill to master; it takes years to acquire that deft touch. Keep that in mind when you're trying to learn how to set—the frustration will end after a few months of practice.

Setting Technique

The best description I've heard of how to position your hands for an overhand set is by Bill Neville, our 1984 Olympic assistant coach. He says that you should put all ten fingertips together, index to index, etc., with your fingers spread wide. Holding your hands down by your navel, push your elbows out away from you. Then raise your hands and arms up above your head so that your hands are in front of your face. Now just pull your hands apart so that a ball can fit nicely between them. You should look through that triangle that forms between your thumbs and index fingers to sight the approaching ball.

Figure 7. Here's how to get your hands into the proper position for setting: put them together, fingertip to fingertip, as shown. Then pull your hands apart so that the ball just fits between them.

The ball should land only on your finger pads, and often it will touch all 10 pads, if only very lightly. Your thumbs, index fingers, and middle fingers are the surfaces through which your wrists really push the ball, while your ring and little fingers just give you extra control. The ball should never hit your palms. If it does it's going to be called an illegal contact.

These days you see many different styles of setting. Some people hold onto the ball longer than others. Some people hold their elbows way outside their body line, some hold them close to their chest. But they all have two things in common. As the ball falls into their hands, they'd like to have loose wrists and stiff fingers. The fingers guide the ball in the proper direction, while your wrists provide a trampoline effect where the ball forces them down, then springs out again.

If you've watched a player like Dusty Dvorak set the ball, you've seen him hold onto the ball longer. That's not bad, it just means that he has supple wrists, not that he's doing something tricky with his elbows. No matter how supple the wrists may be, a setter's elbows always start at a certain angle and extend straight up through the ball, forcing the hands to do the same. A player's elbows should never bend to allow his hands to drop toward his body in an effort to cushion the ball—that means he is holding onto the ball too long. I say this because I see so many beginners trying to imitate a soft, expert touch by flexing their elbows. Avoid this at all times.

Then compare Dusty's style to that of Jeff Stork. Jeff has a style much closer to the older, purer art of setting, where players didn't hold onto the ball as long. Yet he too can make the ball come out with no hint of spin, and can make the ball go anywhere he chooses. Both styles are equally effective, and neither offers a clear-cut advantage over the other.

In the end, you have to find what's most comfortable for you. Emulating either of those setters would be a very helpful start, though. Then you can adjust your arms if you like to hold them wider or narrower, and adjust your wrists if you would like to hold onto the ball longer or less long.

The Setter's Position

In the previous chapter I said that the perfect pass should end up about 12 feet from the right sideline and 1 or 2 feet away from the net. At the beginning of each play, the setter should go to that position and wait for the pass.

You might say, "But I thought there were rotation rules in volleyball—how can a setter legally move to the frontrow from any other position?" The rules state that *before* the serving contact is made, all six players have to maintain their proper positions. *Afterward,* anyone can run anywhere (as long as no one from the backrow hits or blocks in front of the 10-foot line). Even a backrow setter can run to the net to set the ball.

Figures 23–26 (in Chapter 7, on basic team offense) show the setter's various starting positions and how he might get to the ideal target. The setter has a long way to go from some of the starting positions—when he starts in the left back, for instance. The best way to make this move is to sprint straight toward the target, keeping your eye on the approaching serve the whole way. You should be able to get to the net and stop by the time the passer touches the ball. The only time you might be late is when a jump-serve comes over the net—it will arrive so quickly that you might still be moving when your teammate makes the pass.

On defense, the play is often much less organized, and the setter's job is more difficult. He has to be ready to set the ball from any position. For instance, if the coach asks him to block at the left front, and then someone else digs the ball, the setter has to dash back to the target, or wherever the ball goes, and start the offense.

The Setter's Repertoire

This is a good place to describe the different types of sets you'll see or be asked to make. First of all, a *frontset* is any set that goes in front of the setter (toward the left side of the court) and a *backset* is, obviously, any set that goes behind the setter (toward the right side of the court).

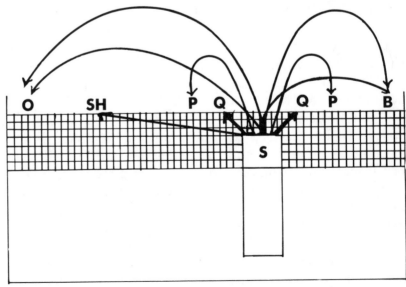

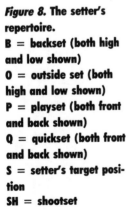

Figure 8. The setter's repertoire.
B = backset (both high and low shown)
O = outside set (both high and low shown)
P = playset (both front and back shown)
Q = quickset (both front and back shown)
S = setter's target position
SH = shootset

The most basic is the *high set.* This is any set higher than 15 feet, depending on what your hitter prefers, out to the left antenna. A *high backset* would be, obviously, anything above 15 feet behind the setter to the right antenna. (There are two antennas on any volleyball court, extending three feet above the net and set up perpendicular to the sidelines.)

Any time the setter jumps up to meet the ball, it's called a *jumpset.* Our coach wanted our setter to do this every time for two reasons. The first was that the ball had to travel less distance to get to the quick-hitter, so the play was speeded up and the margin for error was reduced. Second, with the setter touching the ball at nine feet instead of six feet, he was always a threat to tip the ball over the net on the second contact. Even when the setter was in the backrow, and not eligible to attack from the frontrow, opposing blockers would forget and jump with him.

A *quickset* is a very low set, one to three feet above the net, depending on how high the hitter jumps. The ball is delivered to the hitter when he's already in the air. A quickset ends up about a foot or two away from the setter, who should be standing at the ideal pass location, 12 feet from the right sideline and 1 or 2 feet away from the net. If the pass isn't right on target, though, the quickset should still be placed right next to the setter. A back quickset ends up a foot or two behind the setter. The hitter should always be waiting in the air to draw the attention of opposing blockers.

Shoot-sets are a type of quickset. Again, the hitter should be waiting in the air for the set, but jumps about 10 feet away so that the setter has to "shoot" the ball to him. Teams don't run many back shoot-sets because they are too difficult to time.

As the quick-hitter descends to the ground, an opening is often created because a blocker has jumped with the hitter. Sets created to take advantage of these openings, called *playsets,* are only a little higher than quicksets (three or four feet above the net). Teams often run playsets to the same area as the quickset, or even to other parts of the court.

A *backrow set* is just that—a set to the backrow hitter. It can be any height and location, whatever the hitter wants, as long as it allows the hitter to jump legally (behind the 10-foot line).

The Setter's Role in the Offense

The most important and the most difficult set a setter has to master is setting high to the strong, or left, side. This is because whenever that particular set goes up in the air, the opponents have extra time to prepare to block. When facing two or three blockers, a hitter needs a great set. This often happens when your team has just scrambled to make a defensive play and has an opportunity to score a point.

Being able, from 30 feet away or farther, to place that set 3 feet from the net instead of 10 can be the difference between winning and losing. Especially if a short hitter like me is trying to score that point against a big block.

When receiving serve, a team's offense is much more structured and better prepared to attack. The setter must be even more accurate when these point-scoring opportunities arise. A team must convert at least half of its scoring opportunities if it wants a chance to win. Players must have that killer instinct to turn points with authority every time they get a chance. This is how one team can grind its opponent down. Consistent, accurate setting plays a crucial role in this process.

For smaller teams placing high sets accurately is even more essential. Those teams don't block many balls, but they generally play better defense which earns them more scoring opportunities. Shorter players need better sets to score against bigger blockers.

Sometimes teams rely too much on one or two spikers, ignoring a varied attack. If the match runs long, these players will be too tired to contribute near the end. Setters should involve everyone in the offense, seeing to it that each hitter gets a reasonable diet of sets on which to feed. Relying on one hitter also lowers a team into a rudimentary, predictable offense, and the opponent can anticipate the set to stack up three blockers every time.

Another concern for setters is to keep track of which three blockers are on the other side of the net. If there are two huge players and one who can walk under the net standing up straight, find the short one. On the other hand, if the opponent has no glaring weaknesses, don't be afraid to go at the biggest blocker—he won't be expecting it. A good setter always stays two or three steps ahead of the opponents, eventually making them resort to a guessing game if they are to block any balls.

Finally, setters need to be able to adjust continually to changing situations as a match unfolds. You may feel like you're overloaded with the number of decisions you have to make. Don't worry, with repetition you'll learn to make many of those important decisions instinctively.

If a setter is totally engrossed in a match, as he should be, that attention can cloud his judgment. The coach needs to play a critical role as detached observer and advisor. Which hitter has been most effective in the last game? What about the last four points? Who's been the most effective against this team in the past? In the last game? How about this rotation? Which blockers should the setter avoid and which should be attacked? A coach and his staff should evaluate and reevaluate these trends throughout the course of a match and feed their most pertinent observations to their setter.

Drills

To hone your location skills, set up a hoop, about five feet in diameter and with a net to catch balls in. Center this hoop at the point at which the perfect high set should fall, about three feet away from the net, two feet inside the sideline—and about five feet off the ground. Set 20 high sets at a time, trying to make each fall into the net. At first do this off a perfect pass. As you improve, have the coach vary the passes until you are running all over the court and still able to set 10 out of 20 high sets into the net.

Here's a drill to teach setters to be ready to set in any direction. Have a tosser throw good passes to the setter (who stands at the net) and wait until the ball is almost in his hands before yelling "Front!" or "Back!" to make the setter set forward or backward. See how long you can force the setter to wait. Then vary the location of the tosses to force the setter to establish a good ready position anywhere on the court. If your offense is designed to let the hitters call what set they want, this drill can teach the setter to listen and respond to those calls.

Setters can learn to use their peripheral vision better in a variation of the drill that uses visual cues. The setter stands at the net, a tosser feeds him good passes, and a pointer stands on the other side of the net where the opposing middle blocker would stand. This pointer waits until the pass is descending and then points so the setter can react accordingly, setting forward or backward. With practice the setter should be able to see the pointer's arm without taking his eyes off the ball.

A drill that combines quick decision-making, varied sets, and conditioning is one I called "Setter Frenzy." Three lines of hitters, on the left, middle, and right sides, approach for various sets within the offense, all at the same time. For instance, the most basic offensive pattern we had was the left-side hitter approaching for a high set, the middle hitter approaching for a quickset, and the right-side hitter hitting a backset. The left- and right-side hitters keep approaching and backing up until they receive a set. The middle hitters approach to hit and then run under the net, whether they get a set or not. The coach tosses balls to the setter, at first good passes, and later at varied locations, tossing as soon as the setter has released the previous ball. The setter sets randomly so that all the hitters have to be ready every time. The drill should go 5 to 10 minutes per setter. Our coach would often order the setters to jumpset each time to make the drill even more demanding.

The most common problem setters have is accuracy. First of all, face the target. Whenever a pass comes off the net, setters often make the mistake of not turning their bodies to face the left antenna, no matter where they stand. Many times they'll be in the process of turning as they set the ball, making the ball drift toward the net or elsewhere. Also, make sure you use your arms and legs to guide the ball and follow through with both hands pointing toward the target.

The other common problem is when beginners get frustrated because they don't have the beautiful soft touch of a Jeff Stork or Randy Stoklos. Don't worry—it takes years to acquire that kind of dexterity. If your touch seems harsh, that's natural, and it's not illegal at all. Stick with it.

3

HITTING: "GO FOR IT"

We've arrived at the glamour phase of volley-ball: hitting (also called spiking or attacking). This thunderous technique is what most vol-leyball fans love to watch, and, like the slam dunk in basketball, a great spike can bring an audience to a frenzy, during the warm-up or a match. A variation of the spike is the jump-serve, or spike-serve, which can be equally effective. Both require a player to bring a great deal of horizontal momentum (the approach) toward the descending volleyball, and transfer that momentum upward (the vertical leap) to allow the player to contact the ball at the highest point possible.

Hitting breaks down into four basic elements: the approach, the jump, midair contact, and the tactics and strategies used for different situations.

The first part of the attack is the approach. The approach is the path you take to get to the descending set. The sole purpose of the approach is to position your body, at the high point of your jump, about six inches behind the ball and just high enough to reach it with your arm stretched straight upward. The normal, correct steps in the four-step approach (for a right-handed hitter) are right . . . left . . . right-left. (Left-handers should reverse this.) Use this approach no matter what type of set you are hitting. Very few players can be effective hitters with a "wrong-footed" approach, that is, for a righthander, left . . . right . . . left-right. The first step is for timing and direction. The second step is really the power step that gets you accelerating into the jump phase. The last two quick steps are the plant, preparing for the jump.

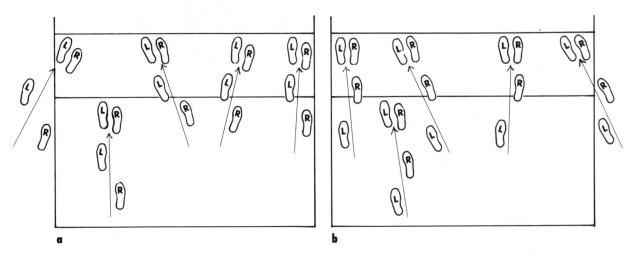

Figure 9. **The four-step approach to the net from different parts of the court, for both right-handed (a) and left-handed (b) hitters.**

When to begin your approach depends on how high the set is. The higher the set, the later you can go. Ideally, you should try to leave late and run faster because the faster the approach the higher you jump.

The approach, or specifically the way you plant your feet before jumping, also helps you to face your body in the correct direction. As a right-handed hitter hitting on the left side of the court, you would like to be facing the cross-court or angle spike. A good way to force yourself to do this is to swing your approach four or five feet outside the court so you automatically arrive at the net facing the angle.

The reason you face this direction is that your body is not built to have a great deal of strength hitting to your right, outside your body line. Nor is your body built to take that kind of abuse.

On the other hand, if you are facing right (the angle), you still have the option to turn your body leftward and hit down the line with force. So always jump with your body facing the angle from the left side and the line from the right side if you are right-handed. Again, flip everything over and do the opposite as a left-handed hitter.

A few more things about the approach. If you are hitting a backrow set, a quickset, or a spike-serve, you must broad-jump. By this I mean you must jump from one spot and propel yourself through the air as far as four or five feet toward the net. There are several different reasons why. For a backrow set or a spike-serve, you broad-jump because you want to contact the ball as close to the net as possible. The closer you are to the net, the more steeply you can hit the ball toward the opponents' court. In both the spike-serve and the backrow attack, you are prohibited from jumping from in front of a line (either the 10-foot line or the endline). So jump from behind the line and travel forward. If you ever saw Steve Timmons hitting a backrow set, you might have noticed how he landed just a foot or two away from the net. In essence he was hitting a normal frontrow set because he could travel so far through the air. That's why he was the best backrow hitter in the world from 1984 to 1989.

If you are hitting a quickset you should jump from five to seven feet behind the net and travel toward it. This permits the setter to see you and your flight path much better. The setter can then deliver the ball to you with much greater precision. Al Scates, the coach at UCLA, is a master at helping quick-hitters with their approach. I could never believe the difference a broad-jump can make.

There's no secret to jumping itself—just jump by pushing with your legs and pulling your arms through and upwards as hard as you can. How high you get depends on how powerful your legs are and how tall you are, among other factors. As you crouch to jump, your knees should bend to an angle of about 90 degrees. If you don't crouch down enough, you won't get full power from the jump. And if you crouch down too far, jumping becomes too slow and the momentum gathered from the approach is lost.

Make sure to use your arms. You do this by swinging them back as you crouch down while planting. Then swing them forward and upward as you jump, to help you jump higher. For some

a   b   c

Figure 10.

players, the height at which they contact the ball will be above 11½ feet; for others, it will be below 8 feet.

Now that you are in the air, what do you do? First you need to coil your body up to hit the ball harder. This compression phase is much like using a bow and arrow, both literally and figuratively. Literally, your spiking arm draws back, and your off hand sights the ball. Your upper torso twists and bends back. And figuratively, these moves prepare you to hit the ball, just as pulling an arrow back readies it to spring from a bow.

Now explode forward to spike. You throw and twist your torso forward, which gives your body torque. The triceps extend the arm forward, the wrist snaps, the hand contacts the ball. The closest analogy in sports is that of a tennis serve, where the server twists sideways and snaps forward to hit the ball. The twist and arm extension give you power. The wrist snap and hand position let you control the direction and the placement of the ball. The ball should be hit with an open hand because it has more surface area for control. Hitting with a closed fist is too erratic.

Where on the ball do you make contact? Imagine the ball as a clock (fig. 11). If you want to hit the ball straight ahead, your contact point should be at 12 o'clock. To direct the ball to the

d   e

Figure 10. This series of five photos shows some of the most important elements in good hitting.
   a. Using your approach to get yourself in the right position to hit the set.
   b. Planting your feet and crouching to get maximum height on your jump.
   c. Keeping your eye on the ball and drawing your arm back to prepare to hit.
   d. Exploding forward to contact the ball.
   e. Following through with your hitting arm as you descend from your jump.

right side of the court, you must hit the left side of the ball, or between 10 and 11 o'clock. To spike the ball to the left side of the court, hit the right portion of the ball at 1 or 2 o'clock. By sighting the ball correctly, you can hit the ball wherever you want.

Figure 11. **Contact points for spiking.**
Contact here to make ball go right.
Contact here to make ball go straight.
Contact here to make ball go left.

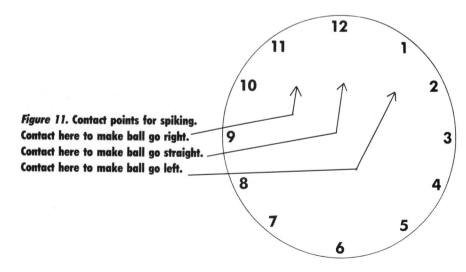

Most players worry about how high they jump, or why they can't jump higher. More important than how high you jump is making sure you contact the ball with a fully extended arm at the top of your jump. Some of the best hitters I've ever seen only needed to jump 12 inches. For instance Tomasz Wojtovich from Poland was a great attacker and blocker but he never needed to jump very high. Instead he used great peripheral vision to see and exploit the opposing block every time. Aldis Berzins was another good example. He never had outstanding leaping ability, but he could always hit the ball with a fully extended arm at the highest point of his jump. This is all any hitter will ever need to do, no matter how tall he is or how high he jumps.

For a normal set you should hit the ball about six inches in front of your head. For a set that is farther away from the net, though, you need to hit the ball from over your head to get it up and over the net. That makes the ball loop more so that you can keep it in the court. And, obviously, when you're closer to the net you can contact the ball farther in front of your head.

Once you've made contact, your follow-through should be in your body line, not outside your body line. What does that mean? Just as a baseball pitcher worries about mechanics in order to protect his arm, so must a volleyball player. For a right-hander, swinging in your body line means following through by your left knee and back up under your left armpit.

Don't forget to land on the balls of your feet with your knees bent. Cushion your landing as much as you can to keep your joints healthy.

Strategy

The perfect strategy would be to spike the ball over the opponents' block every time. Fortunately for all of us smaller blockers, spiking over the block doesn't happen very often because all players have to direct the ball downward. Otherwise, every spike attempt would sail out of bounds. This brings me to the first rule of good spiking: always hit the ball so that, if untouched, it will land in the court. To do this, hit the ball with your whole hand, and snap your wrist. This way you can impart much more topspin to the ball to make sure it travels downward. Watch Adam

Johnson or Scott Ayakatubby the next time you get a chance. They both have great wrist snap and textbook armswings. The ball visibly dives downward as it travels away from them.

You have to hit the ball in bounds. This is because you never know when the blockers might accidentally move their hands out of the way. Your primary goal is to finish the play and win the rally. By hitting the ball in bounds you constantly force your opponents to play the ball, and very often they will not be able to control it even if it's not hard-driven. If you hit the ball out, you've taken your opponents off the hook. Don't make it too easy for the other team. If you gave your opponent a free ball every time by keeping it in play, you would at least have a chance to block or defend to score your points. You lose this chance if you make an error.

The second rule of good hitting is to communicate well with your setter. Make sure to keep all of your comments positive— if you don't keep your setter happy, he will never want to set you. You, as a hitter, need sets so that you can help your team more, because a team with five pretty good hitters is better than a team with two very good hitters. You are also responsible for knowing what particular set your setter has called for you to hit. Once you find a good hitting rhythm, by getting a substantial number of sets, you'll be tough to stop. And your confidence just keeps feeding off itself as you play better and better. Be nice to your setter. You can only find that rhythm if he keeps you involved in the offense.

Tactics

There are three basic tactical plays once you are in the air waiting to hit the ball. All three are important to master—avoidance tactics, attack tactics, and zero-equals-one tactics.

Avoidance Tactics

The first group of tactics is what I call avoidance tactics. As you look up toward the ball, you can use your peripheral vision to see where the blockers and defenders are. First you look for an opening in the block. This would be either an angle shot open to hit, or a line shot that the end blocker is not protecting, or a seam between two blockers. Thanks to our USA offense, I often got to hit against poorly formed blocks. One of my favorite shots was hammering the ball between the two blockers. If the block is well formed, then another avoidance tactic would be to use the same motion as for a normal attack and then tip (this shot is also called a dink) the ball over the block at the last minute. This off-speed shot is effective because, if you use the same motion, the defenders are often back on their heels in anticipation of a hard-driven ball. Pitchers in baseball use off-speed pitches to "keep the hitters honest." In volleyball we use them to keep the defense honest.

Attack Tactics

The next group of tactics is attack tactics. If the other team sets up a strong block then go up and hit it as hard as you can at their fingers. If you hit the ball high enough, most of the time the ball will bounce off their fingers, over the heads of the backrow defenders and out of bounds. Or the ball will rebound backward over your head and out of bounds. We call this "high flat" shot because you are hitting with a flat trajectory, just grazing the opponents' hands with the ball. By hitting the ball harder you can also force it through the blockers' hands so that it will drop, untouched, behind them.

If you are hitting near either sideline, a great play is to hit the ball very hard toward the end blocker's fingers or hands so that the ball will rebound toward the bleachers. We call this a "tool" shot because you have used your opponents' body parts as tools to direct the ball out of bounds. This is also a smart shot because most of the time the end blockers are shorter than the middle blocker, so you are attacking weakness instead of strength. If the opposing player jumps well, you can aim for his forearms instead. A blocker can turn his hands inward to prevent a tool shot, but cannot control the direction of the ball rebounding off his forearms or wrists.

Another variation of the tool shot is best used when the set is very close to the net. In this case you should push the ball forward until you feel the blocker's hands touch the ball, then try to steer it out of bounds. This play starts out looking like a tip.

Using an open hand gives you great control over where you want to place the ball. For that same type of "trap" set you can push the ball down into the blocker's chest if you see that there is space between the net and the blocker. Just push the ball with a quick shove into that space. The ball will go down to the floor before the blocker lands.

The final attack tactic is used when there are weak defenders in the backrow on the other team. If the other team has a couple of lummoxes back there, you can usually assume that they are a liability just waiting to be exploited. So attack at them. Either by hitting, or with off-speed shots, or with a tip, you must make them handle more balls than the better defensive players.

Zero-Equals-One Tactics

The third tactic is what I call "zero equals one." This is perfect for those occasions when the set is in a poor position, the block is in a good position, and/or you have made a bad approach. All you do is tap the ball lightly into the blockers' hands so that it returns right back to you or your teammates. (Imagine playing tennis against a backboard and hitting the ball softly so that it comes right back to your racquet.)

The ball is left in play—a zero on the statistics sheet. But your team has an easy free ball—one more chance to run a whole new play. Your teammates have to be ready to control this type of shot, but when they are, the end result is often a better play.

So what do you do if you are the main hitter for your team, you have been using every shot in your repertoire for the last three hours, and you now have a set in the air that can be put away for the victory? This is no time for tricky off-speed tactics. The other team wants to win just as badly as you do, so it will probably control any off-speed shots or tips on sheer determination. This is what we call "bombs away" time—the time to bring out all of your power reserves, to dig down deep inside of yourself for every last bit of strength, and put everything you have into the ball.

We played like that at the Seoul Olympics. You can compare it to sharks smelling blood. The blood drives them crazy—when we smelled victory, we got wild, too. Near the end of most of our big matches, we were all hitting as hard as we could. That's the way we guaranteed points for our team. Sometimes this tactic will backfire if you get blocked. But how would you feel if you dinked, and the other team picked the ball up and went on to win the match? I would feel as though I hadn't given it my best effort. If one of us got blocked, we would at least have a chance to play the ball again. Just go for it on championship point.

Drills

First of all, hitters need to coordinate all the elements of the approach: the four-step move, the plant, the knees bent, and the arms drawn back. One way to practice this is to take four-step approaches to the net, jump, backpedal, and repeat in sets of 10. See how when you run faster, you jump higher, by getting your eyes above different squares on the net. Or look through or over the net at an object in the distance each time. Another drill omits the backpedal so that you approach and jump from all six positions in the rotation, circling back to the next position after each approach.

Late in the match, instincts often take over when you're hitting. There are some drills, however, that can help hitting become more natural for you. One of my favorites is very simple—it's set up to teach you how to direct your spikes anywhere on the court. Set up a couple of chairs, one in the deep angle zone and one down the line. Both of the chairs can be sitting on the ground or they can be sitting higher, on a box. For this drill we usually had one setter and four hitters on the court—two hitters shagging and two hitters spiking. The hitters alternate hitting a total of 20 or 30 left-side high sets at the line chair. They count how many times they hit the chair. In our case we could only count a successful spike if it knocked the chair over, because we had to practice hitting for power, not just accuracy. Then the other group of two spikers takes the same number of attempts. Whichever team wins gets to rest while the losing group does 50 push-ups.

Then both groups take their turns at trying to bombard the angle chair. I enjoy practicing this shot especially because you can hit so much deeper on the angle than you can down the line. If you practice hitting high and deep enough, you will be able to hit over the block more often in actual competition. Hitting the angle shot over the block and getting power on it is one of the most difficult shots for any hitter to master. One of the best at this shot was Pat Powers—he could often hit right over the world's biggest blockers.

The progression of this drill is to learn first to spike with accuracy, then to hit with accuracy and power so that even if the defender guesses where you're going to hit, he or she won't be able to control it. Plus it's a fun way to compete with your teammates to see who has the best placement when hitting.

A good way to practice swinging high and deep is to hit the ball against a wall—but not the way most players do it. They hit the ball by their ear and bounce it straight down onto the floor. Don't ever practice spiking straight down—you'll get a chance to do that every blue moon. Stand about 30 feet away from a wall, throw the ball up to yourself, and hit it so that it lands on the floor just before the wall and ricochets back to you. Or stand 30 feet apart from a partner and spike the ball back and forth without letting the ball bounce on the ground. Then repeat both of these drills while throwing the ball up higher so you have to jump and hit your own set against the wall or to a partner.

To learn to hit against a blocker, set up a hitting line with one setter and one blocker. Have the blocker either take the line or block the angle every time. The hitters should "hit 'em where they ain't" and find the open spot. After the hitters master this, the blocker should mix it up—make an exaggerated move to block the line or block the angle, but unpredictably—so that hitters can practice avoiding the block.

To practice spiking against a defense, set up three diggers, one setter, and one hitter on each side of the net. One hitter spikes against the other hitter (they alternate trying to block each other one-on-one) while the other four players try to dig. Play all the balls out and see which team's hitter can be the first to win 10 rallies. Then switch sides of the court (right to left or vice versa) so that all players practice left- and right-side hitting.

If there are nine players available, another drill to practice spiking for points off digs is this: set up a full defense on one side of the net. Then put a setter with two hitters, one on the left side, the other on the right side, on the other side of the net. If there's an extra player, put him in the backcourt to help the hitters out. The hitters have to alternate hitting high sets against two blockers. To score one point they must kill three straight high sets off passes that can be located anywhere on the court. They have to score six of these mini-game points to win the drill, and they switch sides (left to right, and vice versa) after finishing half the drill (scoring three points).

For the defense to win, it has to stop the hitters, by blocking or by digging and putting away, 20 times. So the hitters have to score 6 of their points before the defense scores 20 regular points. You'll be surprised how closely this drill finishes, often coming down to the last play when the hitters have scored 5 mini-game points, they have two kills in a row, and the defense has 19 points. The next ball then wins the game for either team.

One of the most common problems hitters have is that they hit the ball long (beyond the endline). This is especially prevalent with beginners. Part of the problem stems from the hitter not being high enough in the air: he doesn't jump well, he doesn't hit the ball at the top of his jump (he mistimes his jump), or both. If possible, take some videotape of yourself (or have a coach or a teammate watch) to see if you are approaching at the right time.

Another cause might be that the hitter is not reaching with a fully extended arm. Many times when hitters are trying to put extra heat on the ball, they drop their arm and hit the ball at about ear level. Realize, though, that the longer the lever your arm forms in its path toward the ball, the faster your hand will move, and the harder you will hit the ball. Again, look at pictures or videotape to see if your arm is straight at contact. If it's not, practice hitting with a straight arm at a wall about 30 feet away. Make the ball hit the ground just before the wall.

Yet another source of the problem might be in your wrist snap. If you get no topspin or, even worse, put backspin on the ball instead, it will sail long rather than dive down in bounds. To strengthen your wrist snap, do wrist curls with dumbbells or barbells. Then stand away from a wall and, keeping your arm straight and stationary above your head, throw the ball up to your hand and practice snapping it toward the wall with your wrist only. Consciously cock your wrist back and snap it forward into the ball.

If you get frustrated, don't give up—there's nothing quite like that feeling of a successful spike that lands on your opponents' floor untouched.

4

BLOCKING
WITH
AUTHORITY

A solid block acts as a catalyst. It scores easy points with stuff-blocks (blocks that terminate play), intimidates opposing hitters, forces errors, helps the defensive players, and can help you take control of the match. In short, strong blocking makes good things happen. But blocking is probably the most neglected skill at every level of volleyball.

Because many teams have neglected their blocking skills, they've really hurt their chances at becoming a better team. Our USA team is a good example. In the early eighties, we were a very poor blocking team. Then, we spent a lot of time working individually and as a team on blocking, and by 1984 we were proficient enough at blocking to be the best team, overall, in the world. Seeing how much easier blocking well makes the game gives players the incentive they need to work even harder for improvement.

The goal, first of all, is to touch the ball every time the other team attacks. It would be unrealistic to think that you could stuff-block every play. If you could, your team would win 15–0 every time. If, instead, your team can touch every ball, then some of those will be perfect blocks, others will be errors, and many will keep the ball in play and increase pressure on the opposition.

The ready position is very important. You should stand a comfortable distance off the net, about 12 to 15 inches. If you're too close, you don't give yourself any room for maneuvering sideways or upward. If you're too far away, you'll allow the ball to fall between you and the net. You've got to try your hardest not to let that happen. So find a comfortable distance from the net—each blocker finds his or her own preference.

You should be on the balls of your feet with your feet spread wider than shoulders'-width; your feet must be set fairly wide so that you have enough leverage to push off and gather momentum toward either side. If you aren't well-balanced on your feet, you won't be able to react toward whichever direction the opposing setter guides the ball.

Your arms should be extended above your head. That is, your hands should be up high (higher than your ears) and in front of your head so that they remain in your peripheral vision. This is so you can react as quickly as possible to the other team's offense. If your hands were at your sides, it would take too long to push them up and over the net. By the time you got to the top of your jump, the hit would already have gone by you. Your eyes should be on the setter as you wait for the pass to fall into his or her hands.

This stance is the same no matter at which position along the net you are located. Look at some pictures or videos from recent USA team tours. The players should always be in the proper ready posture.

Now let's backtrack a bit. If you've scouted your opponents ahead of time, you will know which offensive patterns and which players they will run at you. So as you step up to the net to block, you should call out, first of all, how many hitters there are. Then point out which players are the hitters. It's extremely important to communicate with your teammates, especially the other blockers. Tell them whether the setter is eligible to attack (whether the setter's in the frontrow) and point out the other two hitters. Our typical calls are something like, "Two hitters, middle and right, watch the setter tipping," or "Three hitters, straight across."

As the pass falls into the setter's hands, your arms should now be almost straight above you. All of your attention should be focused on the opposing setter, because no matter where all of the spikers go, they can't do anything without a ball to hit. Who gives them the ball? Only the setter, of course. So always be looking directly at the setter. This doesn't mean that you should ignore the hitters—with practice you should be able to watch them with your peripheral vision even as you concentrate on the setter. Look for clues: if the setter is bent backward, this might give away a backset; if the setter receives a pass a few yards off the net, he will probably have to turn and face the direction where the ball will be delivered.

To start, let's pretend that this set will be going to your area without you having to move your feet at all. This is the easiest type of block because no footwork is required. If the setter sets a quickset (in which the hitter is already in the air waiting for the set) you just take a small jump. That's all you'll have time for and that's all you really need. The vast majority of the time, the attacked ball crosses only a few inches above the net. Remember that you are waiting with your hands and arms almost straight above your head. So it should take just a little hop to get your hands above and a few inches across the net, which is all done in one motion. This is called reaction blocking, because you react to the set. You don't guess where the set will go and you don't let yourself get faked out. The Polish team's players were masters of this system at one time. They didn't block huge numbers of balls perfectly but they kept many balls in play and made it easy for their teammates to play defense. Remember—the object is to try to touch every ball.

Footwork

For all other types of blocking, you'll have to move your feet or time your jump, perhaps both. When you move your feet you'll have to push off your right foot if you want to go left, and off your left foot if you want to move right (it's the same principle as in turning on skis). If you don't believe me, try standing up for a second and moving left by pushing off your left foot. See what happens? Nothing. If you moved like that every time you blocked, your teammates behind you would have to wear crash helmets and seat belts to play defense.

Let's look at the various types of footwork. The first is called a "two-step" move. This is a good move for going up to a third of the way across the court. To move to your right, you would lift your right foot up while pushing with your left. As you hop to your right, you will plant your right foot on the floor (this is the number-one step) then bring your left foot across to join your right (this is the number-two step) and finally jump off both feet. Reverse this procedure for going to your left. Two things are important in the two-step move. One is to plant your feet right where the set will be falling so that you are in front of the hitter. The other is to make sure that you jump straight up and down. Don't drift sideways in the air. If you drift, you're much more likely to block the ball in that same direction. So if you're drifting you'll direct the ball right into the referee instead of down into the court.

Figure 12. **Two-step block move to the right (a) and the left (b).**

The other main footwork movement is the "three-step cross-over" move. This is for longer distances. To go right, take as big a step to the right with your right foot as possible as you push off your left foot. Then cross your left foot in front (between the net and your right foot) for another big step. This forces you to face sideways to the net, but allows you to move faster. After the big step with your left, leave that foot planted toward the net and bring the right around to join it. You should already be crouched down enough so that as you plant your feet you are beginning your jump. Again take yourself right to the spot where the ball is descending and don't drift in the air—jump straight up and down. Reverse this process to go toward the left. This move is great for all of you blockers that find yourselves hippity-hopping frantically to try to join the end blocker.

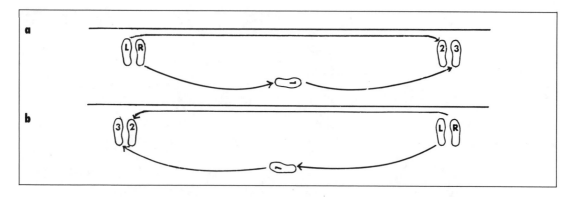

Figure 13. **Three-step crossover block move to the right (a) and the left (b).**

Timing and Hand Position

The other important components of good blocking are good timing on your jump and proper hand position. As soon as you see that the set is not a quickset, you can start moving in the correct direction with the appropriate footwork. By the time the set reaches the top of its arc, you should move your eyes from the ball and lock them onto the hitter. The ball obviously can't go anywhere without a hitter. You're watching the hitter, only watching the hitter, even as you gather to jump. (You're also remembering the hitter's tendencies.) By watching, you will see the hitter's line of approach. Often hitters will hit in the direction of their approach. You will also see which direction the hitter's body is facing—most of the time hitters hit where they are facing.

As you go up into the air, push your hands and forearms over and across the net in the area that you decided to block. Push your hands over if that's how high you jump. Whatever you do, get something across the net. A blocker's cardinal sin is not reaching across the net. Making that mistake allows the spiker to ricochet the ball straight down off your hands and onto your side

a

b

c

d

of the net. That's one of our favorite shots as hitters. If you had been able to reach just a couple of inches farther, over the net, that same error would turn into a perfect block.

As you reach your hands over the net, angle your palms toward the floor and into the court toward the middle back position. When you point them downward you will get more stuff-blocks—and when you point them into the court, fewer balls will rebound off you and out of bounds. Your forearms should be wide enough apart so that a ball might just squeeze through them. Your fingers should be spread as far apart as you can. You've got to cover as much area as you can reach, because the larger the area that you block, the more times you'll touch the ball. Remember, the object is to touch every ball. I consider occasionally letting a ball go between your arms to be forgivable, and preferable to covering too small an area. Steve Timmons has hands the size of toilet seat covers, and once he started spreading them out, he was clamping down on every hitter in sight.

Against teams that hit very high, like Cuba, it's extremely important to reach way across the net. Don't worry about going high. It's just a fact of life that some of the opponents' hits will go over you—but you will still have a large number of opportunities for blocking them because big people try to hit straight down to the floor. And we little people can be very thankful for that. They practice hitting down in warmups, and they'll keep doing it in a game. These are the hits that anyone with good form will block.

I spoke about communication with your teammates before. Often you'll want to tell the defenders behind you that you will block a certain hitter's favorite shot. This frees the defender from covering such a big amount of court space. For example: let's say that a particular spiker likes to hit sharp crosscourt or straight down the line. You and your blocking partner may decide to split-block, that is, to leave a hole between yourselves to take the hitter's two favorite shots. If your defenders in the backcourt know your plan, they will be prepared to dig the hit between the two blockers. We did this against some of the Cuban hitters because they try to hit such radical shots both ways, line or angle.

There are some common errors to avoid. Don't swing your arms back and forth to fool the hitter or to try to cover more area. Just get your hands over and across the net and keep them there

Figure 14. **The first two photographs (a and b) show front and side views of how to start your jump for a block, and the second two (c and d) show where your body, arms, and hands should be at the top of your leap.**

as long as possible. The more you swing your arms around, the more chances you give to the opposing spiker to hit the ball off your hands and out of bounds. And the more chances that your arms will be in the wrong place. For the same reason, you don't want to reach way outside your body line to block a ball. You'll be better off just positioning yourself with your feet rather than reaching with your hands. Against tall teams, many players try to reach very high to block, but remember the rule: penetrate the net. Make opponents hit over you. They can't do it consistently.

I also see inexperienced players closing their eyes as the hitter starts to swing. Keep your eyes open at all times. After spending all that time improving your blocking form, you might as well enjoy watching the ball bounce off your hands and down to the floor.

Drills

Many beginners have trouble with the ball falling between them and the net. This is strictly a matter of poor penetration. To get in the habit of good penetration, squat down on a box or a desk and practice rising up. As your hands ascend above the net, they should penetrate across it also. Then have a practice partner hit balls into your hands in an attempt to sneak the ball between you and the net. Penetrate over to make every ball go back into the opponent's court.

In one effective basic blocking drill, a line of hitters hits only line shots or only angle shots at one blocker. After the blocker has gotten used to this, have the hitters mix it up and randomly hit the line or the angle. Now the blocker has to learn to watch for clues to help him decide what shot to take.

Here's another good blocking drill: one blocker stands on one side of the net with a coach behind him. Three or four hitters stand in a line on the other side of the net. The coach simply tosses balls just over the net for the hitters to attack one by one. The key is that the ball comes from behind the blocker so he can't watch it. The blocker is forced to look only at the hitter. This is not a hitting drill. The spikers should hit straight into the blocker to give him or her practice at making perfect blocks. For a variation, the coaches can toss the ball slightly to the left or right so that the blocker can practice a two-step move to either side. We did this drill several times during the World Cup—it was a good way to get back to basics and improve our blocking, and it obviously worked.

Good blocking can make the game much easier for your team. You can score four or five more points a game with stuff-blocks, intimidate your opponents, and force hitting errors. Blocking is a skill we should never stop trying to improve upon. Blocking is what made winning a World Championship possible for our team.

The key to good blocking is to penetrate the net. The farther you can reach over the net, the fewer options your opponent will have when attacking the ball. The more area you take, the more difficult you make the hitter's task.

5

DEFENSE: NOTHING'S IMPOSSIBLE

At one time, our USA team may have been one of the worst defensive teams in the world. Blocking and defense were our two weakest skills, and we had to make huge improvements in both or we were going to be no better than nineteenth in the world (our finish at the 1978 World Championships). One of my first international trips was to Japan in the summer of 1981. We played a lot of close matches, but we came up with what we call the "big goose egg." That is, zero wins. Why? Because the Japanese played superb defense. They dug our lips off so badly, we couldn't even talk by the end of that tour. It almost seemed as if they were mad at their blockers for denying them more opportunities to dig us.

When Doug Beal, who coached us to our first Olympic gold medal in 1984, put together his mixed approach, he wanted us to pattern our team after the best aspects of the other top programs in the world—to block like the Soviets, attack like the Cubans, and serve like the Brazilians. And he wanted us to play defense like the Japanese. By 1984 we were not the best in the world at defense, but had greatly improved—enough to have won a Triple Crown by emulating the defense of the Japanese.

I think that defense isn't so much a technique as it is an attitude. Many techniques will work. Only one attitude will work—that every attack that crosses the net is playable, that no ball is impossible to get up. Many guys in this country care too much about hitting and too little about defense. But a team can't spike for points unless it can play good defense. The players rotate into the backrow and forget to concentrate on defense, thinking only about the next time they will be able to hit or block. And these days they're also thinking about hitting from the backrow. But will the hit happen if there's no dig or no pass? Not likely. So remember the attitude—nothing is impossible.

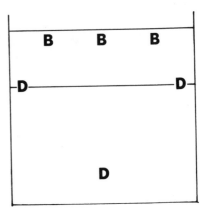

Figure 15. **Defensive starting positions.**
B = blocker
D = defender

Defensive Positions

In the USA team framework, we tried to position our best defensive players in middle back. When the opposing setter is in the frontrow, the starting location for this player is about 6 feet behind the 10-foot line. The middle back has to cover the short area in case the setter dumps (tips) the ball over on the second contact. As soon as you see the set go up (the setter has chosen not to tip) you'll move back with a couple of quick steps to be standing on or very near the endline. That's also where this player should start the other half of the time—when the opposing setter is in the backrow.

From there, you have to be very mobile, since you are responsible for covering the entire width of the court's endline. Even more difficult is the added responsibility of covering all balls that bounce off the top of the block. I loved to play this position, because along with the responsibility of covering large areas I got the freedom to choose my starting location. If you're good at picking the right starting spot, then you'll find many balls coming straight at you.

We had the bigger, slower players line up in the left and right back positions. (The setter plays at right back so he is close enough to the net to set any dug ball.) They're responsible for less court, so they can play with a narrower focus of attention. If you're in one of these positions, your starting spot is at the sideline, just where the 10-foot line meets it. Your outside foot should be a few inches inside the sideline and in front of the 10-foot line. The inside foot is back behind the 10-foot line, so that you are facing into the court. If the spiker hits hard, you would send the ball right back over the net if you were facing straight forward. By facing into the court, you'll keep all the balls on your side of the net.

Our left and right back players are often big enough so that they can fall forward like a tree to pick up balls by the net or in the middle of the court. It's a lot easier to control the off-speed junk, but it's harder to get to. The key for the side players is to stay in position. You can't get scared and flinch backward, you've got to hold your ground. This can be difficult if some huge hitter is about to sledgehammer a ball straight at your face. But we can take consolation in the fact that a volleyball can't hurt you, at least not that much, right?

After you see which side the set will go to, you can take a couple steps back to prepare to dig. If the set is away, you will be looking for an angle shot. If the set goes to your half of the court, your responsibility will be to look for the line hit.

When playing one of these side positions, always stand so that any hard-driven ball from the crosscourt side will be out if it comes above your waist. This gives you an easy test to determine whether or not to play the ball. If you are digging down the line, both of your feet should be inside the court. You don't want to give your opponent a free point by touching spikes that would otherwise have been out of bounds. In the middle back position you are often standing on the endline, so you have to be much more careful in determining whether the ball is going to land in or not.

As the hitter jumps into the air, you've got to keep in mind what his favorite shots are. For example, the great player Alexander Savin of the Soviet Union had one particular tendency. He loved to tip right over the middle blocker. He pushed it into the very center of the court. He did it so often, and so well, that he drove defenses (ours, anyway) crazy. So our two side players tried to lean toward the center of the court. This is very important when a player tips, as Savin did. These balls, if you can get to them, are so much easier to control than a hard spike. Nobody in the world can expect to control a hard-driven ball (anything over 50 miles per hour) from Steve Timmons or Pat Powers much of the time. But any player can control most tips.

If a player likes to hit the sharp angle, then go there and wait for that shot. *Expect* it. Expecting the ball to come to you is an important part of defense. You'll see many players act surprised when the opposing hitter spikes toward them. They're even more surprised when the hitter caroms the ball off the block right to them. Often players misplay these opportunities because they aren't thinking that every ball will find its way to them.

Getting to the Ball

You must be able to innovate and improvise. Although I'm telling you about the best and most effective techniques, there are an infinite number of possibilities to choose from. The best volleyball players are the ones who can improvise in a new situation and succeed. I could tell you what to do in 20 different situations, but your next game might have 10 new ones that I haven't covered. If a new type of play develops, there is no reason to panic. Simply adjust and react to the situation. Action is almost always better than inaction. Along these lines, think of ways to get to the ball: stepping, falling, crawling, diving, rolling, sprawling, jumping, running, and others.

Diving is one of our favorite ways to get to the ball. It seems to be the method of choice among most guys. To learn to dive, start on a gym mat by standing and just lowering yourself down to the mat on your hands, kind of like a reverse hand-stand pushup.

Figure 16. Steve Timmons shows how to go all out on defense.

Land on your sternum—the meaty part of your chest. Keep your chin up to avoid what every player has had at least once: a split chin. Then practice lowering yourself down and pulling yourself through so you slide forward a little.

Next, kneel down on the gym floor and, from that very low position, spring out and land on your chest with your hands pulling through so you slide even more.

After you develop confidence at that, try it with a ball. Have someone toss a ball about five feet away from you, step out with one foot, bump the ball from a low position, and continue through onto the floor. It may help to start diving on the beach instead of the hardwood.

I've known people who could dive sideways and even backward. They had no concern for their bodies, but they made the play. I always land on my chest for fear of injury if I tried to land differently.

Women seem to prefer to roll, probably because of the difference in anatomy. I never learned to roll, and I know I couldn't show you how, but if it works for you, by all means, do it.

Digging Technique

For good defense, it's important to start out in a good ready position. Spread your feet fairly wide. Just like when you're blocking, you'll need to be well balanced for digging in order to make radical moves to either side in reaction to the other team's hits. You should be on the balls of your feet, leaning forward, with your knees bent way down so that you can touch the ground in front of you with your hands. Chances are that you'll have to spring forward rather than backward. Hence the low, forward-leaning position.

Put both arms straight out in front of you, but *not* together in one of the reception grips I spoke of before. Your arms should instead be spread apart and pointing to a spot on the floor about three feet in front of you. The reason that you keep your arms apart is simple. If a ball is hit to one side or the other (which happens most of the time) you only have to move one arm across your body line to meet the ball with both arms. If you were already holding your hands together, it might take too long to move both your arms to either side. Just as when you block, your eyes should be on the hitter, looking for clues as to which way the spike will go and remembering what the hitter's favorite shots might be.

Whenever possible, contact the ball with two arms. This affords you a tremendous advantage in control.

The ideal place to put your dig is high into the middle of the court. Give plenty of time to the blockers so they can get off the net and prepare to hit. You'll also give your setter more time to decide where to set.

When contacting a hard-driven ball with two arms, you often have to absorb the shock, or the ball will spray away out of control. You can do this by falling backward or by pulling your arms back. This is especially true when you watch players receive jump-serves. Look for extra control by acting like a shock absorber for the ball. This also helps the setter out by giving him a softer pass.

Stay low when you play the ball. The Japanese, the players who really set the standard for defense in the 1970s, play the ball as close to the floor as possible. The lower you play, the more

Figure 17. **Remember to get as close to the floor as you can when you're getting ready to dig a hard-driven ball.**

time you have to react. Playing the ball a foot above the floor instead of above your head can give you an extra second or more for control. This is a skill that I learned while playing beach volleyball. This method is great for plays very close to, or under, the net. By waiting on the ground you have extra time to react to the crazy bounces the ball will take as it leaves the net. And, obviously, two arms are always better than one.

Our assistant coach from 1981 to 1984, Bill Neville, taught us to go for low balls that were falling in front of us with a "J-stroke." He wanted us to bend our arms at the elbows as we contacted the ball to help get under the ball and make it travel straight upward instead of forward. By curling your arms under the ball (we called it "J-ing the ball") you can play the ball lower.

Another two-handed technique is what we called the "praying mantis"—named after an insect that looks like it has its two arms locked in front of its head in the act of praying. By putting your palms flat together and then keeping them in front of your face you can dig a high-driven ball. This often happens after the hitter spikes high off your blockers' hands. Another reason we call it praying is that it doesn't work that well. There just isn't enough surface area to control the ball effectively.

You may see players using one arm to play the ball. This technique should only be used as a last resort. If the ball is traveling very wide to either side then you probably have no choice but to stretch as far as you can with one arm. Contact the ball on your upturned forearm, not on your hand. Please use this sparingly, though. I've seen too many times where a critical point was lost because a player was lazy and only used one arm.

Sometimes a ball will be hit so high and fast off the block that you can't turn and run it down. Under these circumstances, I try to jump and stretch as high as I can, and hit the ball upward with one fist. This is another desperation move that should only be used when no other technique will work.

If a hard-driven ball comes way out in front of you, you might try sprawling forward with your hand pointed down, contacting the ball with the top of your wrist. The ball will have to be hard-driven or it might not come up very high. Snap your wrist up if you need to flip the ball higher.

The most spectacular desperation play is the "pancake dig." This dig is used when a ball is falling softly very far away from the nearest defender—and most everybody in the gym thinks the ball is going to hit the floor. The player takes a few steps and dives as far as he can through the air. At that point his body is

Figure 18. The "pancake" dig comes in handy when you can't get your arms beneath the ball from the standard digging position.

laid out horizontally in mid-air, but the ball is still only within reach of one outstretched hand. He presses his hand very firmly onto the floor like a pancake under the ball (hence, the name). His hand becomes part of the floor. Now the ball can bounce up off his hand as though off the floor. It will rarely come up more than a couple of feet off the ground, but you have to do whatever is necessary when you're desperate to keep the ball in play for your teammates. You can practice this by lying on the floor and letting a teammate or coach drop the ball from five or six feet down onto your hand.

The types of plays that I just described, the spectacular saves, are the kinds of plays that can completely turn a match around. I've seen teams like Cuba or Bulgaria fall apart after an opponent made a seemingly impossible play. It's especially frustrating to teams when bigger, slower players make great defensive plays. When the big guys are playing good defense it's almost humiliating to the other team.

That's exactly what happened at the Pan American Games in 1987. We were losing to Argentina 2–0 in the semifinals when Steve Timmons went over the press desk and crashed into the bleacher scaffolding, neck first, to make an incredible dig. Someone set the ball, but I was so worried about Steve—it looked as though he had broken his neck—that I hit it into the net. Even though we didn't win the point, that save inspired the rest of us to hustle more, intimidated the Argentineans a bit, and we went on to win the match 3–2. Don't risk bodily harm (I still tell Steve how stupid he was to go after that ball, and he still tells me I should have hit it over the net), but go ahead—make the big defensive play to help your team win the game.

Drills

The best defensive drills are the most basic: for instance, just a coach on a table hitting over the net at one digger (we called this "coach-on-one"). The goal can be to last a certain time period (one to three minutes) or to make a set number of digs (10 to 30), although digs outside the court or too low to keep the ball in play don't count. The coach should mix in soft shots and off-speed shots all over the gym so that the digger learns to chase down and play balls he never thought he could get to. It's best to have a number of balls so that the coach can hit them rapid-fire.

A good drill we used to learn how to dig hard-driven balls—and not to be afraid of them—was one in which the coach stood on top of a high table about four feet off the ground and the digger stood directly below him. Then the coach hit balls straight down onto the digger's outstretched arms (and made sure not to hit the digger in the face).

Another drill to teach players not to fear the ball is called the "flinch" drill. The digger is positioned wherever he normally plays defense—left, middle, or right back—and a line of hitters simply hits as hard as they can at him. The key is to hit the ball at the digger. Sometimes hitters try to hit so hard that they lose control and the ball goes everywhere but at the digger.

The most common problem among defenders is the dig that goes back over the net or bounces into the stands. To keep the ball in your court, change the angle at which you hang your arms—keep them more horizontal, instead of vertical. And face into the court to keep the ball from going out of play.

You'll also have problems if you are constantly on your heels, backing up, or leaning backward. From this sort of stance, there's no hope that you will be able to move forward to play any soft shots. Make sure that whenever the hitter contacts the ball, you've stopped, established a solid position, and leaned onto the balls of your feet, so that you're ready to move in any direction.

I've thrown a lot of information at you, but don't worry too much about doing everything at once. It takes a long time to break old habits. One rule we had on our team was that there are very few rules. We all learned to react spontaneously to new situations. Sometimes you have to toss the textbook out the window to get the job done. On defense, the best thing to remember is that every ball is an opportunity to make another save—don't ever give up.

6

SERVING: IT'S ALL IN YOUR HANDS

Serving is the one skill that is under your total control. The serve, by definition, is the act of putting the ball in play. You get to do it all by your lonesome. Nobody can affect what you do—unless hostile fans distract you. Your teammates can't make it harder with a bad pass or set. The opponents can't block it. You would think that everyone would be a good server because of this. Just as in basketball free throws are easier (under your control) than shooting from the field. But this is far from what actually happens.

I used to go back to serve with nothing in my mind but, "Please get the ball over the net and into the court." Things really got bad during my junior year at UCLA when an assistant coach tried to make me change my serving style in the middle of the season. At one practice Al Scates, the head coach, told me to serve 10 balls. I only got 2 of them over the net. He told me I could serve any way I wanted to. I just wanted to get the ball in bounds. I needed, as many of us do, to change my attitude toward serving and give myself more confidence.

There are two basic types of serves that the majority of players now use. Both the float and jump serves are worth examining in detail.

Float Serve

At most levels, the majority of serves you'll see are what we call "float" serves. As the ball travels through the air with no spin, it can "float" in any direction, up or down, left or right, depending upon the air currents in the gym and how fast the serve was hit. Not even the server knows exactly where the ball will land—he can only hit toward general targets. Therein lies the advantage of the serve: if the server doesn't know where the ball will land, the receiver can't know. The toughest servers I've faced never served to the same area twice in a row because the ball drifted so much.

There are several ways to hit this serve. One is the Japanese "roundhouse" style of contacting the ball to the side or above the head using a motion where both the draw-back (like a backswing in golf) and the follow-through are done with a straight arm. The movement most analogous to it is a discus throw with a short follow-through. If you are right-handed, stand sideways so that

Figure 19. These photos show the critical stages of the "float" serve.
a. Preparing for the toss.
b and c. With your serving arm drawn back, toss the ball high enough so that you can hit it with your arm fully extended.
d and e. Your follow-through should be short; the idea is not to put any spin on the ball.

a

b

your left shoulder faces the net. With your feet at about shoulders'-width, start by having most of your weight on the foot away from the net, the right one. Hold the ball in front of your chest with your left hand. Your right arm points away from the court, hanging down at a 45-degree angle. (Reverse all of this if you are left-handed).

Throw the ball up so that your arm can swing around and meet it somewhere in front of and above your body. After the ball is in the air, your weight should shift forward so you can hit the ball harder. Just as a baseball pitcher throws harder when he steps into the pitch, you can hit the volleyball harder, making it travel faster, by shifting your weight from your back foot to your front foot as you step forward.

The swing can vary greatly. Some people feel very comfortable swinging sideways, so that they contact the ball at shoulder height or even lower. Others like to contact the ball directly above their head. You should actually make contact with the ball on the heel of your hand. Then follow through toward the court. The follow-through is short because you are trying to contact the ball for a short time only, so it will travel away with very little spin. I wouldn't demonstrate this serve unless I knew people wanted a good laugh. I never learned this technique properly, but if you have a coach who can teach you the style, you should give

c   d   e

it a try. The roundhouse style is very good because it makes it easier to hit the ball with no spin—a "dead ball," as we call it.

The serve that I grew up learning also yields a dead ball. Let's assume that you are right-handed. You will toss the ball up with your left hand as you pull your right arm back, as if you were drawing back a bow and arrow. The ball should be tossed just high enough that when you swing your right arm forward you will contact the ball a few inches in front of your face, as high above your head as your arm will reach.

You're hitting the ball mainly with the heel of your hand, because, again, you don't want to impart any spin to the ball. The less contact area and contact time you have, the better. Not only must you reduce the contact area of the hand, but you also reduce the contact time by serving without following through. You're giving the ball a very sharp, quick sendoff on its way over the net. Your arm should follow through two feet at most.

Serving a dead ball is the first and most important key to effective float serving. Giving the ball more speed is the second key. The faster the ball moves, the more it will change course, sometimes to the point where the other team can't even touch it.

One way to hit the ball harder is to step into it, as I explained in describing the roundhouse serve. You'll have to toss the ball a little farther in front of you, so your body can move forward to meet it.

You can also try to keep the trajectory lower. Once you can control the direction of the ball, it's much better if it clears the net by a few inches, rather than by a yard or more. The ball will travel faster and the opponents will have less time to react. This is why taller players can often serve better than shorter ones, and, by virtue of a lower net, why women can serve tougher than men in most cases. Shorter people can compensate by serving from farther behind the endline, so that the ball is traveling downward by the time it crosses the net.

Don't be frustrated, this is a very difficult art. I still have a lot of trouble making a good float serve.

Jump-Serve

The jump-serve (or spike-serve as it is sometimes called), which the Brazilians popularized during the 1984 Olympics, is the other serve of choice. I like the jump-serve for three reasons: First, it allows a server to put a team on the defensive. I mean "defensive" literally because when it is hit hard this serve is no different than a spike. Second, the serve allows you to disrupt the rhythm of a team that is handling float serves too easily. When all six players are float-serving, the opposition can get into a passing groove because there is so little difference from one server to the next. But when one or two players are jump-serving it forces the other team to adjust back and forth between the two styles of serve. Third, with the jump-serve you can see immediate results: one or two aces at the right times can make a big difference in the course of a match, especially if the server rarely serves aces with the standard float serve.

The most difficult part of this serve, besides serving it in bounds, of course, is the toss. I've seen many different tosses by jump-servers. Left-handed, right-handed, and two-handed tosses are all common. I use my right hand and toss the ball up about 6 feet in front of me and 10 to 16 feet high. Eric Sato, our team's best jump-server, uses his left hand and a much lower toss. Just as with a standing float serve, moving forward to meet the ball gives you more power in the delivery. So toss the ball out in front, and run up to meet it.

Here's an easy way to think of a jump-serve. You've seen players attack at the net, and from behind the 10-foot line, so why not attack from behind the 30-foot line? As long as you jump from behind the 30-foot line (the endline) before you serve, you can land anywhere.

I also toss the ball up with a forward rotation because I feel it helps me to hit the serve with more top-spin, which makes it travel downward into the other court. It takes a long time to learn consistency in your toss. Don't be frustrated—I'm still inconsistent with my own tosses. I'll often hit the ball slowly, just to get it over the net, because of a bad toss, and because I'm afraid to make a mistake.

The farther you move away from the net, the higher you

have to hit the ball to get it over the net. To hit the ball higher, you should contact it more above your head instead of in front of it. Many jump-servers contact the ball behind their head to loop the ball up and over the net. If you hit the serve the same way you would attack at the net, you would hit your own players in the back of the head—or, worse, have it bounce and *then* hit them.

Once, arriving in Havana after a long trip, we went directly

Figure 20. Eric Sato shows excellent technique for hitting the jump-serve.

to the gym for our first match. Steve Timmons was so frustrated (as we all were) about not getting any sleep that he hit his first jump-serve as hard as he could. It hit teammate Dave Saunders in the head and almost knocked him out. After the crowd gave him a standing eight-count, we were well on our way to losing in three straight games. Moral: Put higher arc into your jump-serves, if only to safeguard your teammates' health.

If you must risk error with this serve, risk making it too long rather than too short. Many times receiving players can't decide whether the serve is in bounds or not, because the ball is dropping steeply. So they might play some of those serves. Sometimes they just can't get out of the way of the ball, it's coming so hard. But if the serve hits the net, the other team has not had to make any split-second decisions.

One very important thing the coach has to do is encourage his jump-servers to take a few chances, and allow them to miss more serves than the other players. The other players will have to be prepared for these risks. This is a high-risk strategy, but it can reap quick results.

Eric Sato played this role in the 1988 Olympics. He served five aces for us, even though he was being used as a substitute. Two of those aces were on match point, the second being at gold-medal point against the Soviets. Our coach, Marv Dunphy, told him never to hold back. He gave our team a tremendous advantage because of it.

Serving Strategies

Before picking where to put your serve, you have to remember some guidelines. After the other team has called a time-out, you should make sure your serve goes into the court. Missing your serve at this juncture is a cardinal sin. The other team called a time-out because they had problems, so why let them off the hook by missing the serve? If your teammate before you misses, you should also make sure to serve cleanly. We tried never to miss two serves in a row. If your team has an opportunity to win a game or to win the whole match on your serve, you should also try harder to keep the ball in. But if your team's been stuck on game point for several plays, you might want to take a chance and hit a high-risk, high-yield serve. That way you take the opponents out of their rhythm.

At all other times, you can use less caution to try to hit a tougher serve. When you go back to serve, what should you look for? It will help if you know who the weak passers on the other team are, either by scouting before the match or by your coach telling you who is passing poorly as the match proceeds. The best possible serve would be one that makes the opposition's worst passer move before playing the ball. Even the worst passers are decent if the ball comes right at them. By making them take a step or two, you make their job much more difficult. The best way to make a player move is to serve to the perimeter of the court—a passer always stands toward the center of the court to begin with. If you can serve the player deep or short or toward either sideline, you can make him move more. Another good choice is the area between players, although this isn't as effective because another passer might be better and step in to take the ball.

If none of these strategies works, you can try to change the rhythm of your serve by taking some power off the ball. This way you can serve the other team a ball that is not floating much, but is landing extremely short or deep in the court. What you lose in strength you gain in accuracy. By holding a little strength back, you can deliver the ball with a higher trajectory so it can land just a few feet from the net. You can serve the next ball deep to the endline. This will keep the passers off balance. Craig Buck, the gold-medal middle blocker for our team throughout most of the '80s, was a master at mixing the speeds of his serves. He'd serve hard and deep, then soft and short, leaving opposing passers cringing by the end of a match.

Our team also used another method if we were having trouble scoring points: we would sometimes deliver an easy but accurate serve to the opposing quick-hitter. This can disrupt the other team's offense by forcing the hitter to pass well and then attack. Two jobs are tougher than one.

Here's one more strategy to use if all else fails. Almost all teams run their offenses with their setter standing facing the right sideline (the sideline to your right as you stand ready to serve). And a setter's job is easier when the pass comes from in front of him rather than from behind. So you can try to disrupt a team's offense by serving along the left sideline, in front of their serving area. Even better is a very short serve to that sideline. This way the pass comes from almost directly behind the setter. It's more difficult for the setter to see the ball, the hitters, and your blockers, or to run a smooth offense.

These are some of the tactics that you, the server, have at your disposal. You've also got to have steady nerves as you prepare to serve near the end of a big match.

Drills

To practice serving with a low trajectory, string some elastic tubing from one antenna to the other, about three feet above the net. See how many serves, out of 10 or 20, you can make go between the elastic and the net—without touching the net. Then lower the elastic so there is only two feet of room and practice again. You should learn to make your serves clear the net by only about 12 inches.

To practice serving into seams, mark areas of the court with chairs or with lines on the wood. Mark the corners, the deep middle, and the areas along the sideline. Have contests to see who can land the most serves out of 10 in these areas. The corners can be worth two points, the other marked areas one point, any other legal serve zero points, and any out-of-bounds serve minus-one point.

Another helpful drill is to practice serving into the marked areas in succession. For example, to get out of the drill, you might have to serve into the deep line corner, the short angle, the deep middle, the short line, and the deep angle corner, all in a row. Switch the order on other days.

To put even more pressure on, make the entire team, one player after another, complete a set pattern of serves before anyone can leave practice. This is like having all the members of a basketball team make 50 free throws in a row at the end of practice.

The most common problem that servers have is not getting the ball to float. One reason might be that the server isn't serving the ball without spin. Remember to rap the ball with the heel of your hand as quickly as possible so that you don't put spin on the ball. Practice serving knuckleballs softly into a wall about 5 feet away. Then slowly move back until you are serving from about 30 feet away, about the distance the net would be.

Another reason serves don't float is that the trajectory is too high. You can hit lower-trajectory serves much harder, and they'll move or float farther. Lower your serves with the elastic-tubing drill I described earlier.

Try to learn several types of serve so that you can serve tough and change the rhythm of a game if things are not going well for your team. These techniques take a great deal of time to master. Just go back and think about serving tough, concentrate on it, and you'll start creating more opportunities for points as the other team has trouble handling your serve.

7

THE BASICS OF TEAM OFFENSE

No matter what level of volleyball you play, the real rewards come when you and your teammates assemble the individual skills we've been working on to create the best *team* possible. It's very special when you make plays that you never thought could be done—these are moments that I live for (at least *on* the court!).

If you're even luckier, you'll play these special matches during important tournaments. Whether you're playing your big rival, playing for a league championship, or playing for the World Championship, there is nothing like the feeling of having your team's play "come together" during a big match. I hope the next few topics—on team offense—will help your team feel that euphoria when it all "clicks."

The Evolution of Team Offense

One of the things that makes the sport of volleyball so challenging is that both teams play offense *and* defense on every play—

Figure 21.
The 3-3 offense:
possible starting positions.
S^1, S^2, S^3 = setters
A, B, C = hitters
underline indicates
a frontrow
position

and often have to switch from one to the other in the blink of an eye. For example, as soon as a serve crosses the net, the serving team switches from offense (trying to score points or sideout) to defense. Once the receiving team passes the ball successfully, *they* switch immediately from playing defense to running their offense. Both teams have played both offense and defense *before* the ball is returned back over the net.

Volleyball offense wasn't easier decades ago, but it was less complicated. One of the offenses used by teams then was what we call a 3-3, in which there were three hitters and three setters. The lineup alternated hitter and setter around the court. Each

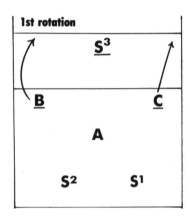
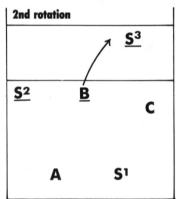
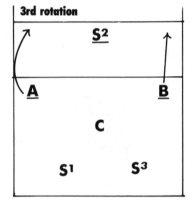
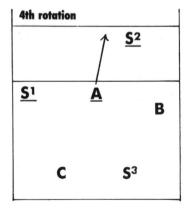
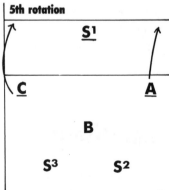
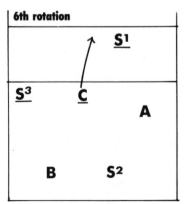

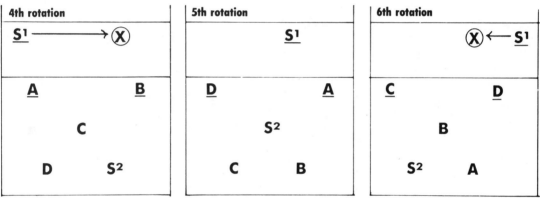

hitter was paired with his or her own setter. This exclusive relationship improved teamwork in the offenses, but the 3-3 limited the repertoire to high sets on the left side or high sets to the middle. Backsets were rare, so one frontcourt hitter was used in each offensive rotation. One hitter offered little chance for deception—and gave the defense a big advantage.

Then came the advent of what we call a four-hitter, two-setter offense (4-2). This is the first offense I learned, in junior high school, and it's still a sound offense for many teams today. In the 4-2, the two setters are situated opposite each other. Whichever setter is in the frontrow pilots the offense, leaving two frontcourt hitters and doubling the setter's choices. De-

Figure 22. The 4-2 offense: possible starting positions. Note that these diagrams show how the setter should get to the setting target from each starting position.
S¹, S² = setters
A, B, C, D = hitters
underline indicates a frontrow position
x = passing target that setter should move toward

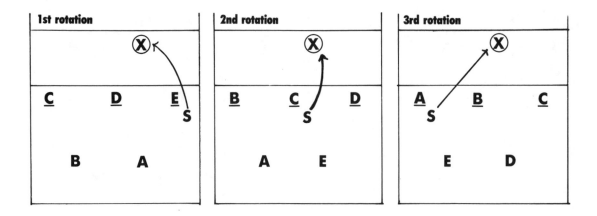

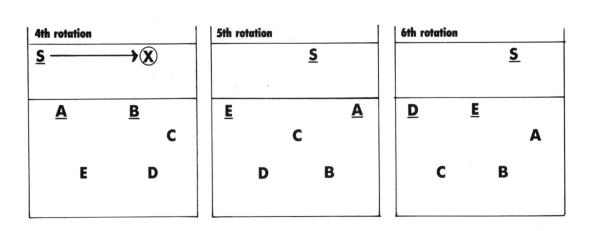

Figure 23. **The 5-1 offense: possible starting positions. Note that these diagrams show how the setter should get to the setting target from each starting position.**

S = setter

A, B, C, D, E = hitters

underline indicates a frontrow position

x = passing target that setter should move toward

pending on the setter's position, he or she could choose between a frontset and a backset, or a frontset to the far side and a low set to the middle. The system allows more variety, but since only two hitters face three blockers, the offense is still at a disadvantage.

After the 4-2 came the five-hitter, one-setter (5-1) offense, and the six-hitter, two-setter (6-2) framework that I played in during college at UCLA. Both of these offenses allow a team (although only half the time in a 5-1) to use three frontrow hitters at a time. Three hitters versus three blockers. And the blockers can only guess at where the set will go. Advantage to the offense? Definitely.

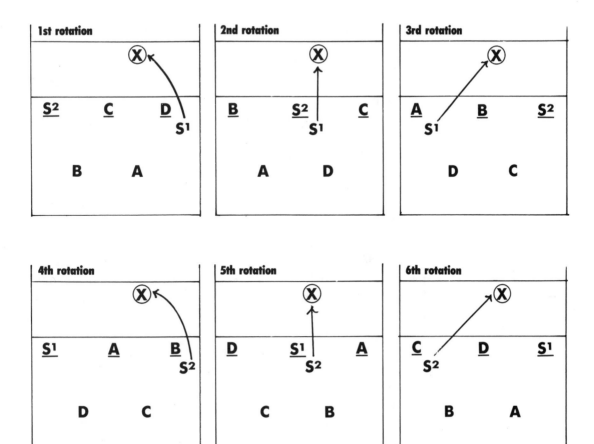

Figure 24. The 6-2 offense: possible starting positions. Note that in this offense, the setter in the front row becomes a fifth hitter.

S^1, S^2 = setters
A, B, C, D = hitters
underline indicates a frontrow position
x = passing target that setter should move toward

The 5-1 offense is what almost every top international team and most top collegiate teams play. It allows the setter to specialize in doing what he does best—to set every ball. The scheme forces the setter to master his art, and it allows him to learn the nuances of each hitter's style—where and when he prefers the ball. The 5-1 does have a disadvantage: whenever the setter is in the frontrow (three out of every six rotations), there are only two frontcourt hitters, instead of three. Most teams make up for this by using backrow hitters—the backcourt attack is now an integral part of many teams' offenses. Lately, I've seen high school teams use the backcourt attack with greater skill than many international teams brought to it in the early 1980s. (See the following chapter for a discussion of adding your own backrow attack.)

The 6-2 offense uses six hitters and two setters (placed opposite each other in the rotation). This sounds like eight total players, but it isn't, because both setters also hit. That is, whichever setter is in the frontrow hits, while the backrow player sets, so that each setter hits in half the rotations, and sets the other half. Although this offense gives a team three frontrow hitters in every rotation, the two setters only get to set half as often as the 5-1 setter. As a result, 6-2 setters are often only about half as good as 5-1 setters.

The 5-1 and 6-2 schemes allow a team to use many types of sets and plays. High, medium, and low sets to any spot on the court. Quicksets in front of the setter, where the hitter is waiting in the air for the ball to be delivered just out of the setter's hands. Back quicksets behind the setter. Shoot-sets that travel along the net away from the setter. Double-quick plays with two hitters, one approaching in front of and one behind the setter, or both in front. Playsets that go into the same area as a quickset, using the quick-hitter as a decoy. Playsets that go to other areas of the court. Pump-sets with the hitter faking a jump to get the blocker into the air, and then jumping up and attacking as the blocker falls to the ground. Backrow sets to different areas on the court. Using three or four hitters at a time, the permutations are endless.

Keys to a Championship Offense

You should have three basic goals in putting together your team's offense:

1 · To receive well, getting an accurate pass to the setter
2 · To give the hitter a well-placed set that will be easy to spike
3 · To place that set so that the hitter is operating against the weakest block and defense possible

Once you have these three elements in place, you'll be able to run an effective offensive on every play.

Passing

No offense, even the most rudimentary, will work without a good pass. Show me a team that can't pass and I'll show you a losing team. Show me a team that passes well, and I'll show you a successful team—maybe not one that wins every game, but certainly one that will have fun trying.

A bad pass gives your offense only one option: to pray that your setter can make an extremely difficult set, and that your hitter can put the ball away on the left side against a three-man

Figure 25. The "W" passing formation (five passers).

P = frontrow passer

P = backrow passer

S = setter

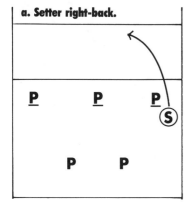

a. Setter right-back.

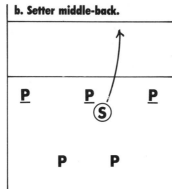

b. Setter middle-back.

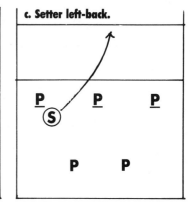

c. Setter left-back.

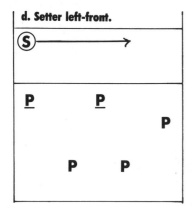

d. Setter left-front.

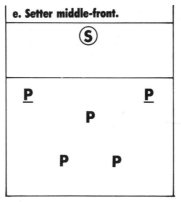

e. Setter middle-front.

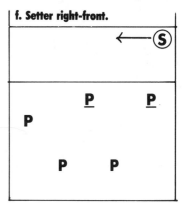

f. Setter right-front.

Figure 26. **The "cup"**
passing formation (four
passers).
<u>P</u> = frontrow passer
P = backrow passer
Q = quick-hitter
S = setter

block. No team has the talent to do this consistently—so learn to pass the ball!

The basic serve reception pattern for most teams is the "W" formation (figs. 25 a–f). All five passers—everyone except the setter—prepare to bump the ball to the ideal target. I mentioned that target in the bumping chapter: 12 feet from the right sideline and 1 or 2 feet off the net. After the serve, the setter runs up to the target, waits for the pass, and sets the ball.

Once a team attempts to use quicksets, though, it has to relieve the quick-hitter from any passing duties so he can get into the air on time. These teams usually use four passers in a cup formation (figs. 26 a–f). The most vulnerable area is then the

Figure 26. The "cup" passing formation (four passers).
<u>P</u> = frontrow passer
P = backrow passer
Q = quick-hitter
S = setter

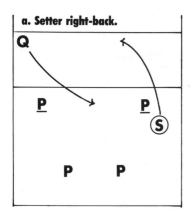

a. Setter right-back.

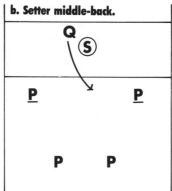

b. Setter middle-back.

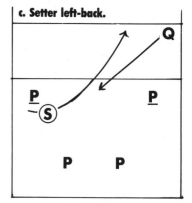

c. Setter left-back.

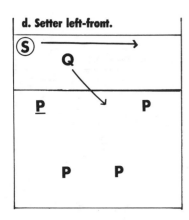

d. Setter left-front.

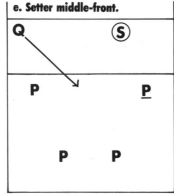

e. Setter middle-front.

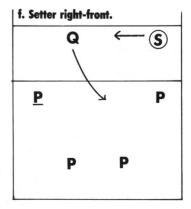

f. Setter right-front.

short middle area, and the team must clarify in advance whose responsibility that area is. For instance, the short area could be covered by the left and right front passers. Or, if the backrow passers are mobile enough, maybe they can cover that territory.

In both of these schemes, all the passers should make sure to call out who will pass the ball. And not only call it, but confirm it just so everyone knows. For example, if I were in the right front position, and the serve was coming at me a little high, I would say, "I've got it!" And the passer behind me would confirm by saying, "Yes, yours," or "Karch." Or, if he thought he had a better shot at it, he'd say, "No, mine!" Then I'd have to reaffirm by saying "Okay." This way everyone on the court is sure about who is doing what. If two players call for the ball at the same instant, they should keep talking until they are both sure who will play it. It's always better to have two people there instead of one.

If your team can't receive service well, you may not be able to set, period, let alone get the ball to a good spot along the net. In fact, if your team can't pass you might want to consider running the archaic 3-3 offense I mentioned earlier. Teams that want to start running quicksets had better remember that no pass equals no offense. You can't run quicksets from the 10-foot line!

Offense: Basic Options

Once a team is passing well and setting accurately (see Chapter 2 for a thorough introduction to successful setting) it can concentrate on its third fundamental goal—delivering the set against the weakest block and defense.

Aiming at the weakest block can be as simple as setting toward the shortest or weakest blocker (although shortest and weakest aren't necessarily synonymous). It can also mean the ultimate in setting—giving your team's hitter a one-on-none opportunity. (Hitters cherish one-on-one opportunities only slightly less.) A weak spot in the defense can also be a digger leaning backward—leaving space for a tip to fall in front of him or her—or, better yet, a defense that leaves gaping holes into which your hitters can make easy putaways.

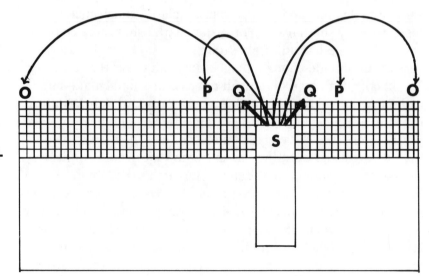

Figure 27. The offense's basic options.
S = setter's target position
Option 1. Q = quick-hitter (front or back)
Option 2. P = playset hitter (front or back)
Option 3. O = outside hitter (front or back)

Taking advantage of these weaknesses depends on your set-ter's ability to find them—and then to get the ball to the hitter who is in the best position to take advantage of the opportunity.

Your setter has three main options: to set the quick-hitter; to set a playset hitter near the quick-hitter; or to set a playset hitter far away from the quick-hitter. Keep reading—I'll explain how these options work *and* how your setter should decide be-tween them.

The setter's first option is the quickset. Building a sound, complete offense depends on developing your team's ability to run quicksets. Setters have to become confident in running these sets at any time, even during the most important plays, the set points and the match points. The constant threat wears down opposing blockers and gives them some difficult choices to make. Hey, I would get tired just watching our quick-hitters. Having an effective quick-hitter like a Steve Timmons waiting in midair, ready to launch missiles for hours, forces the opposing blockers to do one of three things: they can quit trying, which happens more often than you'd think; they can give the hitter a large advantage by waiting on the ground to see exactly where the set goes (this is called read-blocking); or they can have one blocker jump with the quick-hitter wherever he approaches (this is called commit-blocking).

The setter's next option is to set a playset. The effect of a playset is like two pistons moving in opposite directions. The quick-hitter jumps up, drawing a blocker with him or her. As they descend, the playset hitter jumps up and hits the ball, before the blocker has time to jump again.

The setter's last alternative is to set high outside. We called this the "outlet" because we often used it when no other sets would be possible. If someone shanks the pass, then the only place to set is high outside.

Again, the setter is the key to this process. Your setter has to be able to discern whether your opponents are read-blocking or commit-blocking—and set the options accordingly. Let's take a closer look at these two basic situations.

Case #1: Blockers Are Reading

Let's look at the case where the opposing blockers are read-blocking (waiting on the ground and reacting). The setter's first choice would be to set quick, because nobody is in the air to oppose it. Play the percentages. If all the blockers stand on the ground 100 percent of the time, the setter should go quick consistently throughout a match. Not predictably, but often. It's a big advantage for the setter to keep the other team guessing, often guessing wrongly, and that means using a variety of sets throughout a match—but in this situation the setter should always be thinking of setting quick first. Many teams follow a different pattern: set quick early, then forget about it. But they also allow the opposing blockers to forget about the threat.

The setter's other choice would be to set away from the quick-hitter or "against the flow." Often the quick-hitter's mere presence and movement will draw the attention of the blockers. Those blockers have to move so that, at the very least, they stand in front of the quick-hitter—otherwise they would have no chance of stopping him or her. As one or two of the blockers move with the quick-hitter, the opposite side of the court opens up. If the quick-hitter goes in front of the setter, the playset should go the other way, some distance behind the setter. This way the offense is spread out along the net, and the blockers are forced to cover the whole width of the court just to get to the point of attack.

Even the best teams in the world can't run the same play all of the time. For example, in the basic X-play (which we'll discuss in the next chapter) a quick-hitter approaches in front of the setter for a quickset, while the playset hitter comes right afterward to hit a set just marginally higher. The quick-hitter draws the attention of the blockers—so they all lean toward him to defend. If the setter opts for the playset, all of the blockers are already leaning in the right direction, and they aren't forced to move their feet in order to block. They can and often do get three blockers up—now the offense is at a disadvantage. So spread your offense out against a team that is read-blocking. Use the whole court, "from pin to pin" (antenna to antenna), as Bill Neville used to say.

Case #2: Blockers Are Committing

On the other hand, if the opposing team is commit-blocking, many of the sets should go away from the quick-hitter. This is because one of the blockers assumes that the quick-hitter will get the ball, and jumps all-out to stop it, taking himself out of the rest of the play. Even in this case the setter should sometimes set the quick, because it is a one-on-one matchup—and the advantage still belongs to the spiker.

The greater advantage belongs to the playset hitters, though. The other two blockers are left speculating as to which hitter will receive the set. Those blockers are often left alone to block one-on-one. Any hitter will tell you how he or she would love to hit one-on-one every time. If the other team is commit-blocking, the playset hitter probably has the best chance to put the ball to the floor.

The commit-blocker is also an obstacle around which the other blockers have to move or reach just to get in position to block. With the commit-blocker hung up in the air, the best place to run the playset is right over him. This would be setting "with the flow," setting a playset tight over wherever the quick-hitter goes, and just slightly behind, so the playset hitter has room to jump and swing. The basic X-play is a good choice here. Or use the back-X (also discussed below), where both hitters approach behind the setter.

We had a series of drills designed to help the setter get used to making these choices. One drill had a quick-hitter and playset hitter attack at two or three blockers and try to kill 15 balls before the blockers stop them five times. The blockers can commit all the time, or read all the time, at first, and then mix up their schemes as the setter becomes more proficient. Ideally, the setter would set quick whenever the blockers don't commit early. But this is impossible to do 100 percent of the time, unless the setter has a third eye in the side of his head. If the setter can make the correct choice most of the time, he or she is doing a superb job.

Since the setter can't always see what the blockers are doing, another system was invented (by the Polish team) wherein the hitter—instead of the setter—makes the choices of playsets. The hitter watches the opposing blockers to see whether they are read- or commit-blocking, and calls the playset accordingly. The disadvantage of this system is that the control of the offense is taken away from the setter, who's supposed to be a lot smarter than the rest of us hitters, right?

Our USA system used a combination of these two offenses. Off serve reception, our setters, Dusty Dvorak, Jeff Stork, and Ricci Luyties, did the play-calling. In transition, the hitters did most of the play-calling. We didn't like to call more than one play at a time, so as the rally continued, the hitters were free to make new choices on each attempt.

I can boil this basic offensive concept down to two sentences. If the blockers always wait on the ground, set quick. If they jump a lot, set away from the quick-hitter, either playsets or sets to the outside. That should make it simple for you to run an effective offense.

Drills for a Basic Offense

The most basic team passing drill is to set up the serve reception pattern and serve balls at each rotation. To succeed, each rotation might have to pass 5 or 10 perfect passes in a row—then go on to the next rotation until all six are completed.

Most of the other drills we did on the USA team combined the whole sideout game—passing, setting, and attack. (This makes sense because only rarely is a play completed without setting and hitting.) Remember that the most important element in team passing is good communication. Players can never, ever talk too much during a play. Practice calling the ball on every play. The whole team will determine who will pass, there will be no confusion, and the pass will be perfect.

Another basic drill sets up the offense against a full defense of blockers and diggers. The offense has to win one rally off serve reception, and then three to six more, all in a row, off free balls. The coach has to decide how many times this has to be accomplished per rotation (maybe one to three times), and then the team has to perform this in all six rotations to finish the drill.

Another drill changes the numbers. The offense has to win three plays in a row off serve reception while the defense has to win just two in a row. The coach decides how many times this needs to be done to win each rotation (maybe one to three times), and all six rotations should be contested. Or the two teams can play to six—that is, the first team to win six rotations wins the drill. We called this "3 versus 2," or if the offense was really playing well, "4 versus 2."

A variation of both of the above drills is one where the offense has to win 4 or 5 plays in a row off serve reception, while the defense just has to win a total of 10 plays. For example, if the offense wins three in a row, the score is 3–0. If the defense then wins one, the offense goes back to zero and the score is 0–1. This way the drill can't last all day. The offense can only fail nine times.

To teach the offense not to make errors, to keep the ball in play, try this drill, where the offense has to win 20 free-ball plays, scored plus-or-minus. That means that if the offense loses the play for any reason, by mistake or because the defense made a good play, the offense loses a point, and goes backward. We sometimes even played that the score for the offense could go into negative numbers; one time I remember the offense falling to minus-7 before eventually getting to 20.

Some drills force both teams to play offense and defense. A famous one from the USA team is the "wash" drill. One team serves to the other team, then receives a free ball. That way both teams get one chance on offense. One team has to win both plays or the whole point is a wash. No matter what happens, the serve alternates, that is, one team starts by serving one wash, and the other team starts serving in the next one. A team has to win both plays to earn a point, and has to win four to six points to win a rotation, and has to win 6 to 12 rotations to win the drill.

The wash drill can be modified to make it more difficult for one team. For example, the A team, or starting team, might need to be challenged more. So the drill would consist of the A team receiving serve, then defending while the B team gets a free ball, and then receiving a free ball on a third play. The A team has to win all three in a row to garner a point, while the B team only has to win any two in a row, the first two or the last two. If the B team wins the first play and the A teams wins the second play, the play stops and starts over (becomes a wash), because neither team can accomplish its goal of two or three in a row. To win a rotation, either team may need to win by two to six points, depending upon the coach's mood that day.

In all of these drills the coach should remember that the offense has the advantage—it wins about two-thirds of the time. Our offense was playing well if we gave up less than one-half of a point per rotation. That means that each time the other team served, we won two sideouts for each point it scored. Therefore, any drill set up should be biased against the offense, like the "3 versus 2" drill above.

In any of these drills, the coach can put constraints on either team. For instance, he can make the A team set quick at least 50 percent of the time, to practice the quick offense. He can make the A team run only a certain series of plays to hone a particular skill. He can make the A team set the backrow one out of every three plays. Or he can even make the B team run a certain offense to mimic what a particular opponent does.

I hope this section has given you a few ideas on how to run the offense. Remember again, pass the ball first: every good offense flows from that. Practice until your offense becomes smooth—master putting the ball away against the second team, and things will become much easier during the games.

8

ADVANCED TEAM OFFENSE

Now that we've covered the basics of setting up an effective offense, I'd like to introduce a few of the complicated wrinkles that are being added to today's most potent offenses: the many variations on basic plays, the addition of a backrow attack, and the two-man passing game. Before we get into these offensive schemes in detail, though, let me give you some guidelines on how teams can best use their talent.

Setting the Best Rotation

First, try to figure out who's going to set. As I said in Chapter 2, the setter is the most important position. Although it's the most critical choice, it's also an easier choice than deciding where hitters should play—in the middle or on the outside. Which player is the best setter is usually pretty clear. But it may take a long time to figure out where each hitter can be most effective— on the left side, on the right side, hitting quicksets, hitting play-sets, or even attacking out of the backrow.

There have been players who have joined the USA team still unaware of what their full spiking capabilities are. Before settling on a lineup, coaches should force hitters to try a variety of positions.

Finding the best places for these players in the rotation is something that takes a lot of thought and some luck. For instance, if a team has a great backrow hitter, it should use him when the setter is in the frontrow and only two other frontrow hitters are available. Should that backrow hitter be opposite the setter or two positions away? If he's opposite the setter, he can hit backrow in every rotation where the setter's in the frontrow.

The coach should draw out all six rotations in each of his possible lineups and analyze their strengths. Evaluate how well each rotation might sideout (a measure of offensive strength), how easily the plays or the players can be switched if the offense is struggling. (Remember, after the serve, players can switch positions sideways: for example, after the serve, the right-front player can go to the left-front and vice versa.) Assess how well each rotation might score points, through serving, blocking, defensive play, and putaway power off the dig. Then look at what substitutes are available, and go through the entire process again, assessing what might be added by bringing other players into the game.

Often the two tallest players play opposite one another, blocking middle and hitting quick, although that is not a hard-and-fast rule. The two best passers usually play opposite, hit outside, and pass. A lineup like this would then place the setter in one of the remaining positions, with another strong hitter opposite him.

The next consideration is which quick-hitter should be next to the setter and which should be two positions away. Usually the better quick-hitter should play next to the setter, to make the two-hitter rotations (when the setter is in the frontrow) stronger. The same goes for the choice of outside hitters.

In a two-setter offense, the two setters should play opposite one another; so should the two big quick-hitter/middle blockers, and the two all-around players at outside hitter. The placement of the players is usually less critical than in a one-setter offense, since a coach can always flip or switch the two players playing the same position in the lineup.

Basic Volleyball Plays

Next, I'd like to describe some of the basic plays used by most teams today. (An offensive attack becomes a play any time you involve more than one hitter.) These plays are the foundation on which any complex offense is built. All teams have to master these basics to become great, and for some teams, blessed with tremendous physical ability, this is all they need—about three basic, but perfectly executed plays.

The most basic play of all is best known as the 4-1-5. It involves a front set from 10 to 30 feet high, to the left-side hitter, a quickset directly in front of the setter for the middle hitter to attack, or a backset, about 10 feet high, to the right-side hitter. Each hitter stays in his own area, and there is no misdirection or trickery involved.

Before teams start worrying about making an offense more complex, they should think about running variations on the 4-1-5. For example, they should think about having the left-front hitter hit the quickset, while the middle-front hitter swings around to the left for the high outside set, with the backset option remaining the same.

Or how about switching the roles of the hitters in the other direction? You can invent many variations with even the most

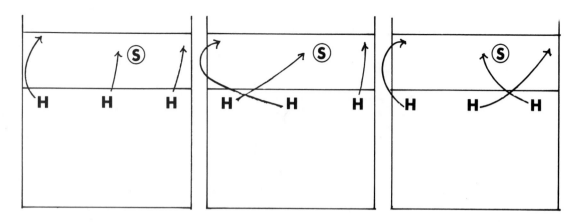

Figure 28. **Three variations on the 4-1-5 play.**
H = hitters
S = setter

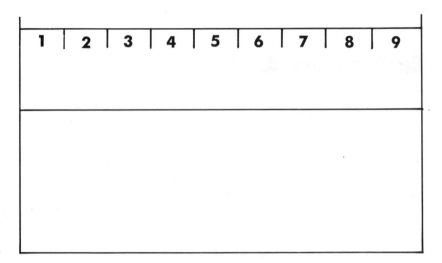

Figure 29. **Set terminology: zones 1 through 9.**

simplified offense. Don't think you need to run the USA offense to win your high school or club championship.

On the national team we used a specific terminology so that every player knew what set we were calling. Divide the court into nine segments (fig. 29) across the court, each about a yard wide, from the left side (zone 1) to the right side (zone 9). The first number in any set destination is the zone. The height of the set, in feet, is the second number. So a 51 is a set in the middle of the court (zone 5), one foot high. A 51 is another name for a quickset. An 11 would be a set to the left antenna, again one foot high. This would be a shoot-set all the way to the left sideline. Not many teams run something like this, but if you were ever to see it, you could now describe it.

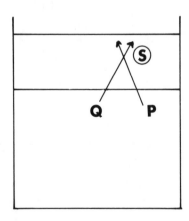

Figure 30. **The X-play.**
S = setter
Q = quick-hitter
P = playset hitter

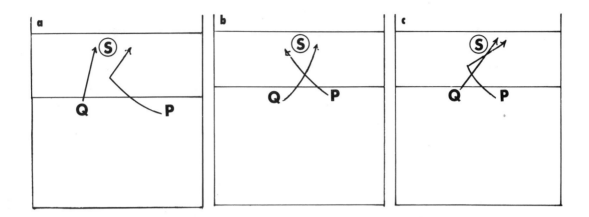

Figure 31. **Variations on the X-play (with the quick-hitter coming from the middle-front position).**

a. The fake-X.
b. The 71-X
c. The 71-fake-X.
S = setter
Q = quick-hitter
P = playset hitter

Using this terminology, we'd call the 4-1-5 play a 19-51-99 play: a set 9 feet high to the left, a set 1 foot high to the middle, and a set 9 feet high to the right. I said before that the left-side set goes from 10 to 30 feet high, but that adds extra digits to the terminology (making it a 110 or a 130 set), so I lowered the sets a bit to simplify it. I'll try to use this to make it easier for you to follow some of the more complicated plays.

The first real play I ever learned, as most players do, is the X-play (fig. 30). This is where the quick-hitter comes for a quickset (a 51) right in front of the setter, and the playset (a set about two or three feet high, a 53) comes to the same spot right afterward. The whole idea of this play is to force the opposing blockers to make a choice. If the blockers choose to ignore the quick-hitter, the setter gives him the ball. If the blockers choose to honor the quick-hitter, and jump with him, the setter can give the ball to the 53 hitter instead. As I mentioned earlier, the play looks like two pistons moving in opposite directions—as the quick-hitter descends, and the blockers descend with him, the playset hitter jumps and quickly hits the ball before the blockers can get back into the air to stop him.

If the opponents start getting the hang of stopping the X-play, your team should run the fake-X (fig. 31a). The quick-hitter goes to the same spot to wait for the set, while the playset hitter fakes like he's coming for an X. At the last second he veers away for a low backset (a 73). Each play is designed by the offense to gain an advantage—in this case the advantage is that the blockers expect an X and lean into the middle of the court to stop it. That should leave the right side of the court open for the fake-X hitter.

With these two plays and little other deception, the Polish team won the 1976 Olympics. With these two plays, the teams I played on at UCLA won three out of four NCAA championships. Any team can win running these two plays skillfully enough. So don't think that your team needs to get any fancier—master the 4-1-5 and its variations, and the two X-plays first, and worry later about adding more complexity.

Variations on the Basic Plays

Another variation of the X is to send the middle-front hitter behind the setter for a 71 instead of a 51. The playset hitter can either go in front for a 53 (figure 31b), or in back for a 73 (figure 31c). These are good wrinkles to add when the blockers keep standing in the middle of the court to stop the 51.

If the other blockers are able to stop those plays, as is unlikely, what should a team do? One option is to run a back-X (fig. 32a). Now the quick-hitter comes from a different area on the court, the right side, and hits a quickset behind the setter (a 71). The hitter in the middle-front becomes the playset hitter, and

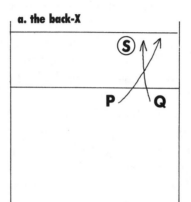

a. the back-X

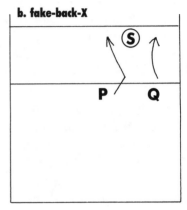

b. fake-back-X

also goes behind the setter for a low backset (a 73, the same as for a fake-X). You can actually create four options from this formation by sending the right-front playset hitter in front or in back (for a 53 or 73) of the setter.

One of the four permutations, a fake-back-X (fig. 32b), is a good choice once the opposition has come to expect the back-X, that is, when the blockers have moved to their left to cover the back-X and vacated the middle of the court. Then the middle-front hitter can fake like he's going to hit a 73, and come back in front of the setter to hit a 53 with nobody in front of him.

Figure 32. More variations on the X-play (with the quick-hitter coming from the right-front position).

S = setter

Q = quick-hitter

P = playset hitter

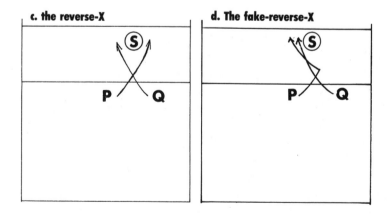

c. the reverse-X   d. The fake-reverse-X

Next, the offense can get the left-side hitter involved by running a tandem play (fig. 33). The quick-hitter goes to his normal spot in front of the setter for a 51, and the playset hitter runs in from the left and catches the other team unaware, hitting a 53. But if the other team has concentrated on stopping the X, this play won't be much different and probably won't be effective.

A whole new series of plays are spawned when a setter can master a shoot-set. That's a set where the quick-hitter waits in the air some distance away from the setter for a very fast set, for example, a 31. Once a team has a good 31 attack going, all sorts of new options become available.

In the series called the 31-X series (figs. 34a and 34b) the middle-front hitter hits a 31 while the left-front hitter hits a playset, a 33 or a 53, behind the quickset. He can go to two

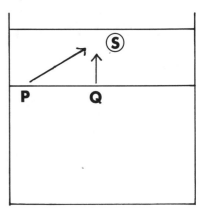

Figure 33. **The tandem play.**
S = setter
Q = quick-hitter
P = playset hitter

different spots depending on whether or not the opposing blockers move way over to their right to try to stop the 31. If they do, the 53 becomes the better playset because again the middle of the court has been vacated.

An easy variation of this is to have the middle- and left-front hitters switch roles: the left-front hitter goes for the 31, and the middle-front hitter goes for the playset.

This is a play the Soviets used over and over again, against us and everyone else, with great success. What made it so effective was their huge quick-hitters. We had to honor the 31 threat every time, or we could never stop it. But we got back at them with hitters like Steve Timmons, Craig Buck, and Doug Partie—we could run the plays equally effectively.

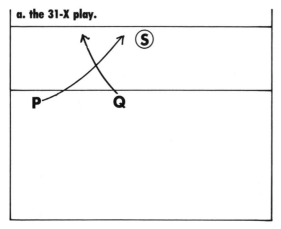
a. the 31-X play.

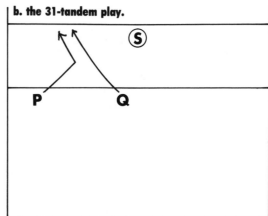
b. the 31-tandem play.

Figure 34. **The 31-X series.**
S = setter
Q = quick-hitter
P = playset hitter

With the block worrying so much about the 31, the right side of the court opens up. Any backset becomes easier to put away. That's often how we were able to open our backrow attack up for Timmons or Pat Powers—off a 31 to Buck.

Another way to open up the backrow is for a team to run all three players in front of the setter—for example, with an X. Usually the three blockers will also move to their left in response, leaving a backset to the backrow wide open.

Things can get even more complicated when two hitters go for quicksets. This is called a double-quick offense, and might combine a 31 and a 51, or a 31 and a 71, or a 51 and a 71.

Adding a Backrow Attack

Now you may be saying to yourself, "Some teams I watch use more than two hitters at a time—they use backrow hitters." Well, you're right. In our 5-1 offense, we had three hitters in the frontrow only half the time. The other half of the time, we had two frontcourt hitters and at least one backcourt hitter, if not more.

Your offense should be running like Swiss clockwork before you even think about attempting backrow attacks. If the passes, sets, and hits aren't flowing easily already, this addition is not for your team. You don't ever want to make things more complicated for players if they haven't already mastered more basic skills. Using a 10-foot-line attack is definitely an advance, but it imposes a new level of complexity on a simpler offense.

There is a paradox associated with supplementing your frontcourt offense with attackers from the backrow. Although you've got to have solid, proficient skills to be able to use it, there must still be some weakness in your offense—or some strength in the opponents' defense—which prescribes the need for a backrow attack. You must be good to use it, but you must have the need to get better if you feel the need to add it. In our case, we felt we needed it to help deal with a very strong Soviet block. We weren't as successful as we'd hoped using only two hitters when the setter was in the frontrow. We couldn't have become the best team in the world without our backrow attack. Steve Timmons and Pat Powers gave us a dimension, actually a double dimension, that no other team in the world could match.

If you would like to use the backrow, you have to start with gifted athletes like Steve and Pat. Or at least one. Don't even attempt to run anything from back there unless at least one player on your team can hit from the backrow effectively. The players I've seen who are very good at it don't necessarily jump well, but it helps. Those players do hit with maximum extension of their arms, and broad-jump a great distance forward. The closer to the net you can hit the ball, the easier it is to hit well.

Another important concept is the placement of the backrow hitter in the rotational order. Ideally the hitter would be opposite the setter, as Pat was for us until he retired in 1986. That way we had at least one backcourt hitter in every rotation where the setter was in the frontrow. If you are fortunate enough to have two backrow hitters, one could be opposite and one a position or two away from the setter.

Earlier I spoke about setting with the flow or against the flow. These same rules apply to integrating the backrow attack into your offense. But before setting up who goes where in the offense, you've got to remember to avoid having the backcourt player approach the same area as a frontcourt hitter. There are two reasons for this. One is that the two players may jump on each other because they can't tell whose set it is. The difference between the two sets is often only a couple of feet—or less. The frontcourt player might like the ball three feet from the net, while the backcourt hitter, when he or she is broad-jumping well, might like it five feet from the net. Steve landed on my back more than a few times when we both went for the same set, and it isn't a pretty or a safe sight. The one exception is that it's acceptable to run a low backcourt set behind the quick-hitter, because there will be no confusion as to whom the ball is for. The other reason for keeping the hitters separate is to add deception to the offense. The more hitters you have bunched into one area, the easier they are to block.

When Doug Beal originally set up our offense, he divided the court into four equal parts along the net (fig. 35). As your team looks at the net, those would be, from left to right: areas A, B, C, and D. We also used a set called a "pipe," which comes from baseball when a pitch goes "right down the pipe" over home

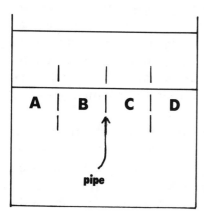

Figure 35. Backcourt hitting zones—A to D and pipe.

plate. Our pipe set went right off the setter's shoulder, wherever he was standing at that time. That was slightly right of the center of the court, because that's where we liked to pass.

You might ask, "Why confuse me with yet another system of terminology?" The answer is that if you describe both front-row sets and backrow sets with the same system, you have to include three pieces of information: the set height, the set location, and whether the set is to the frontrow or the backrow. For example, a 945 could be a set to area nine, four feet above the net, and five feet away from the net. Hitters might get confused, thinking, "Did he say a 941 or a 949? Is that for the frontrow hitter or the backrow hitter?" It's much easier for both the setter and the hitters to use completely different names for backrow sets. With this system, when the setter calls out, "Hit a D," everyone knows that it will be a backrow set.

Here are some examples of what an offense that incorporates a backrow attack might look like. You can send the quick-hitter toward the center of the court, send the other frontcourt hitter toward the left antenna, and let the backcourt hitter go for a D. Or from that same formation you can have the backcourt hitter hit a pipe. The heights of these sets should be as low as possible, because they are really just playsets that go a little farther away from the net. Or you can have both frontcourt hitters go for quicksets while the backcourt player hits an A or a D. You can also send the quick-hitter for a shoot-set toward the left sideline while the backcourt hitter also moves to that side (to hit an A) and have the other frontcourt hitter go behind the setter for a playset. You can see that the possibilities are endless, but again only if the pass is consistent.

Do you see how, in all of those plays, we liked to keep the hitters spread out along the net? This would be the case no matter what type of blocking scheme the opponent was using. If you watched our team, you saw me hitting from the left side most often. The opponents know this (it's predictable). But that left more room for the backrow attacker, Steve or someone else, to hit D sets or pipes.

Some teams even use a backcourt hitter in the three-hitter rotations. This gives them a four-to-three advantage, hitters to blockers. An example would be a normal play where you have a left-side hitter and an X-play. This means that all three frontrow hitters are attacking in front of the setter. So the D in back of the setter is an open spot on the court for a backrow hitter to jump and land in. Teams might do this in order to give the set to the "hot" hitter, the one who is having big success against that particular opponent. This way, you can set the hot hitter in the frontrow or the backrow.

The Two-Passer System

Many teams, in an effort to cut down on the communication required with four or five serve receivers, try to use just two or three instead. Any two- or three-passer system might be modeled after the USA team passing system, installed by Doug Beal in 1983.

The two-passer approach was a big factor in our team's success, but it wasn't an American invention. I first played internationally in 1977 at the Junior World Championships in Brazil, and that's where I learned that a two-passer system was possible. The Soviets astounded us with their skill at service reception using only two players in the common beach-volleyball configuration (fig. 36). They used any two of four different players in that formation. They completely dominated each of their opponents, including us Americans, with ball-control skills I'd never seen before from such tall athletes.

The difference between other two-passer systems and the USA version is simple: we used the same two players to pass in every rotation. In five of the six rotations we were even positioned the same way, with one player (Aldis Berzins or Bob

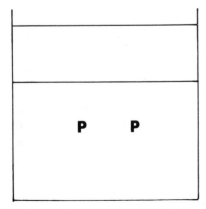

Figure 36. Receiving positions in the two-passer configuration.

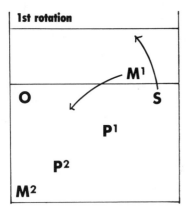

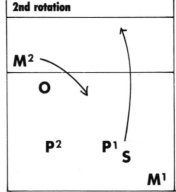

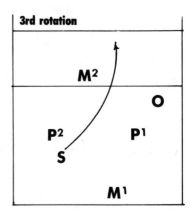

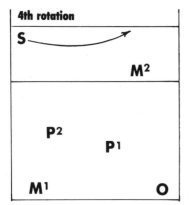

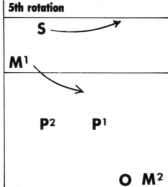

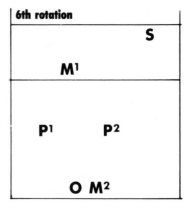

a) Two Passers Opposite

Figure 37. **Two-passer rotations with a) the two passers opposite and b) the two passers two positions apart. Note that these diagrams also show how the setter can get to the setting target from each starting position.**
P¹, P² = passers
M¹, M² = middle hitters
O = outside hitter
S = setter

Ctvrtlik) on the right and me on the left, as we faced the net. So almost 85 percent of the time, the two of us were standing at the identical location when the opposing team served. Other teams had their passers in different locations, with different people surrounding them, in each different rotation.

Despite mandatory rotation and strict substitution rules, players can still be specialists. That's the first advantage of the system—we got to feel very comfortable because we rarely switched positions. More importantly, the system allows two players do the work of five. Five people need much more communication to decide which player will pass the ball. Two people only need one call to figure out who's going to pass. The areas of responsibility are also more easily defined with two people.

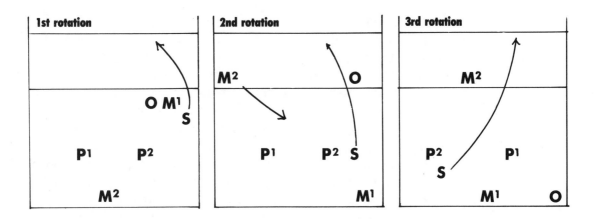

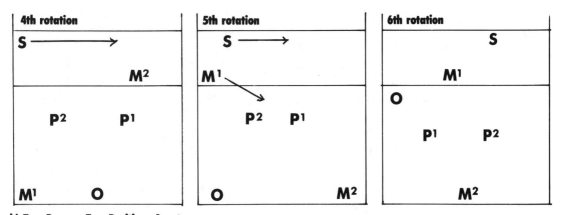

b) Two Passers Two Positions Apart

The two passers can improve their concentration when they don't have to worry about four other players getting in their way. When two players can concentrate solely on passing, all of the other players can help them decide if the serve is in or out and then prepare to attack easily. So the other players can concentrate better, also. The other players are freed from the onus of passing and the passers are freed from them getting in the way.

One of the greatest advantages of a two-passer system is that a coach can use his two best passers exclusively and insure the team a higher percentage of perfect passes. The players who don't pass well don't need to worry that the other team will be trying to exploit their weakness. These players can develop more confidence and concentrate on their strengths.

If you feel that your team has two accurate, mobile passers amenable to this system and would like to try it, here are some keys to making it work. Both passers must be able to stay on their feet at all times because they have to be able to hit immediately after they pass. Although placing the two players opposite one another in the rotation is convenient, it isn't necessary. The coach should draw all six rotations out with each possible starting lineup in mind. I don't know of any players currently on the USA team who could assume passing responsibility for half of the court *and* hit quicksets in the offensive scheme. You'll want the two passers at least one position apart so that you will always have a quickset hitter in the frontcourt—even in a one-setter offense.

Once a coach decides on a lineup, he must have the passers spend a high percentage of practice time (as we did over the years) learning to receive serve and then to hit various sets immediately. First, the players should pass from the left side and hit from the left side; they should then pass from the left and hit playsets in the middle of the court; finally, they should pass from the left sideline and hit low sets at the right antenna. Then the drills should be flipped so that the players can work on right-side passing. In all of these drills, the serves the passer must receive should be progressively more difficult, from easy balls tossed over the net, to easy serves, to, eventually, the toughest serves the other players can muster. Your passers should be able to pass from anywhere on the court and then hit from anywhere else. Because they have extra work passing and hitting, passers in this system have to be in superb condition.

Another key point that players have to learn is when to adjust individual positioning. If your opponent is serving only toward the other passer, you should move over a few feet at a time to attempt to cover more court for him. You can lure your opponent into serving your way by leaving a large piece of court apparently unprotected, only to move back to your original position after the server throws the ball up. I sometimes tried this, since our opponents often served at Aldis or Bob to tire them out.

Sometimes teams tried to serve toward our frontcourt passer exclusively, thinking that they could wear him down since that player would have to pass every time, then approach to hit. We liked this because we knew where every serve would go—the opponents' serving tactics became completely predictable.

The two-passer system tests a player's stamina—that's the system's biggest challenge. If one passer can't last a whole match, his team will lose. That's what happened to our team in August 1983, the last time we lost to Japan while I was a member of the team. It was a four-hour, five-game, 95-degree, 90-percent-humidity fiasco in Osaka. Aldis received almost every serve. After his skin color turned from red to green to white as he got heatstroke, we lost 16–14 in the final game as he missed a few passes. By the end he was so tired he couldn't even speak. That happened soon after we had begun using the system, and we realized that both passers needed to be in better condition.

Having learned from that experience, we prepared ourselves better for the World Cup in 1985. Our extra conditioning turned out to be critical, especially in our epic struggle with the Soviets, when they served every ball at Aldis. He passed about 185 serves that day, compared to the 220 he received over all six matches of the 1984 Olympics. He had to survive three hours and 36 minutes of passing and hitting. That match took a tremendous toll on him physically and mentally, but he lasted and we won. With a lesser player, we would have lost.

The other challenge of receiving with two players is determining which player will take serves that land in the middle of the court. It took at least a year for Aldis and me to figure out who was going to receive certain serves. Even after that, we always called out who was to pass the serve, leaving nothing to chance. Why guess where your teammate is when you can talk to him and find out?

If the opponent uses a hard jump-serve, two players can't possibly cover the entire court area. This is where a three-passer offense is required. If your team faces a strong jump-server, bring in a third passer, preferably to the position least likely to be served at. If the server rarely serves down the line, put the extra passer there.

The three-passer system has also been used by the US women's team. (Women, because they play with a lower net, can serve much tougher than men, and covering the court with just two passers is more difficult.) I think the three-passer system offers some of the same advantages as the two-passer system, but to a lesser degree. If a team wants to have any type of backrow attack, it must free at least one player from passing responsibilities. Internationally, women's teams use a backrow attack less often, so there's not as great a need for systems using fewer passers.

The two-passer system is certainly more difficult at first, but it can be well worth the effort for some teams. Try it and see if it can help yours.

9

TEAM BLOCKING

How can any team hope to score points against a great offense—to block and to dig these 90-mile-per-hour spikes? It sounds like a hopeless job, and over 50 percent of the time, it is. It's just the nature of the beast that the offense, especially with the evolution of backrow attacking, has a huge advantage. After all, only the setter knows where the hitters and the ball will go. And there are always three hitters, sometimes even four, assaulting only three blockers who *don't* know where the hitters or the ball will go.

Most teams build their defensive foundation with a sound read-blocking system. This means having two agile middle blockers who are quick enough to stop even the fastest of sets toward either sideline. All you do in the read system is to react to the set. That means never getting faked out: never jumping when you shouldn't and never leaning one way when you need to go the other.

The opposing setter is the key to the read-block system. All of the blockers focus primarily on reading the setter—looking for clues as to which way the set will be directed. This goes for the end blockers as well. They can afford to lock their gaze on the setter because they have to look into the court to do so, and that way they can still use their peripheral vision to keep tabs on where the hitter immediately in front of them is going.

As the hitters in their periphery move in different directions, the blockers should be communicating. This would sound something like, "He's coming around!" or "X, X, X!" It is really important that the other blockers know what's happening on your side of the court and vice versa. For instance, if you are blocking on the left side and the hitter directly in front of you (the other team's right-side hitter) comes for a quickset, what do you do? You would probably be tempted to jump with him, but if your teammate yelled that there was *another* hitter coming around to your side of the court, you would know that you should wait and react to what the setter does.

In this system, by waiting and reacting after the play develops, you give the other team's quick-hitter the advantage. But as a blocker you can never take away all of an opponent's shots. By keeping your arms extended above your head, you can still touch a good number of the quick-hitter's attacks, because many cross only a few inches above the net. The most difficult move for a blocker is not to move—to wait. When the opponents are running an X-play, you have to wait on the ground. Giving a little to the quick-hitter means taking a lot from the playset hitter. It's a game of calculated risks and percentages, and the keys to it are communicating, reacting, and keeping your hands high.

A tactic that should be used in all blocking systems, but especially in the read system, is that of having your end blockers stand more toward the middle of the court (fig. 38). The end blockers should be at least one big step in from the sideline. On the USA team, we called this "pinching in" the end blockers, and we did it because the middle blocker needed all the help he could get. That way we could often get three blockers up to guard against an X-set, but we could still cover the sidelines when necessary.

The other main blocking system is the commit-stack system. In this, as I mentioned earlier, one blocker jumps (commits) with the quick-hitter no matter where he goes. If the set goes somewhere else, well, then you've wasted a blocker. But if the set goes quick, you have a good chance to get at least a deflection. What happens to the other blockers? One of them has to stand behind (stack behind) the commit-blocker and take up the role of

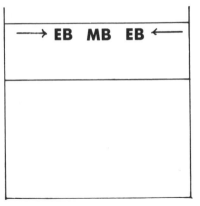

Figure 38. **Pinching in the end blockers.**
MB = middle blocker
EB = end blockers

middle blocker. That means the stack-blocker has to be able to move to either sideline. If he moves to the right, he joins up with the right-side blocker to form a two-man block. If he moves to the left to stop the other hitter, he blocks alone (one-on-one). The stack-blocker's movements are dictated only by where the setter directs the ball. So the stack-blocker is in essence reading the setter, doing what all the blockers were doing in the read system described above.

There are right-side stacks and left-side stacks, among others (fig. 39). If your opponent is running an X-play a lot with a powerful quick-hitter, you would use a left-side stack. Left-side means that the left blocker pulls in to stand behind the commit-blocker. That way the left-side blocker is already in position to stop the X-set. The Soviets use this system almost exclusively, because their premise seems to be to try to stop the quick-hitter at all costs.

What if your opponent uses a shoot-set type of play about 10 feet to the left of their setter? That play is the Soviets' favorite. It would demand a right-side stack where the right-side blocker pulls in and stands behind the commit-blocker. Then that right-side blocker is in a good position to stop the playset, which also arrives about three yards in from the sideline (the right sideline if you are looking at it from the blockers' side of the net). The stack-blocker can also depend on help coming from his left as the left blocker leans in toward the middle of the court.

A more complicated system that some teams use is the double-stack (fig. 40). One player commits on the quick-hitter and the other two blockers stand behind, waiting to react in

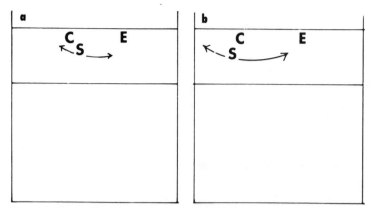

Figure 39. Stack-blocking.   S = stack-blocker
a. Left inside stack.   C = commit-blocker
b. Left outside stack.   E = end-blocker
c. Right inside stack.
d. Right outside stack.

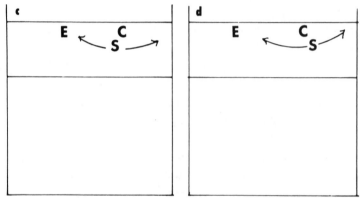

Figure 40. Double-stack blocking.
S = stack-blockers
C = commit-blocker

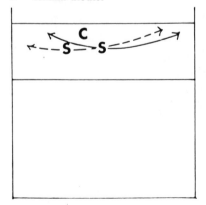

whichever direction the set goes. That might be used when an opponent's offense consists of a quick-hitter in the middle, a regular hitter on their left side, and a strong backcourt hitter on their right side. In the event of a playset, your hope is to get two blockers in front of the hitter who gets the set.

Drills

Players can learn blocking teamwork by having two blockers run back and forth across the court blocking alternating high sets to either side. Have different groups of two go at a time, so that each player learns to block next to any other player.

One drill forces a single blocker to try to stop the X. He should try to touch every quickset and every playset. Then have single blockers work against other plays like the 31-X series, or the back-X series. Then have two blockers work together against the same plays.

To practice blocking systems with all three blockers, set up a controlled offense against three blockers and instruct the blockers to use one of the above blocking systems. To practice against the 31-X series, for example, have the offense run only that series.

Another group of drills is made possible by putting a full complement of diggers behind the three blockers, and setting goals for the defense—say, that it must stop the offense five times before the offense wins 15 plays. At first, constrain the offense to certain plays only, then eventually make it more difficult by allowing the offense to run any play.

I have purposely thrown some very difficult things at you to show you how complex the game of volleyball has become, and is still becoming. If you are able to master these concepts, you can use them in designing your own unique schemes for use against specific opponents—or, if you want to get even more ambitious, against specific rotations of an opponent's lineup.

10

TEAM
DEFENSE

Even if your team had the best six blockers in the world, how good could you be without defense? Although great blocking can touch and deflect many attacks, the majority are not repulsed. Or look at it from another perspective: how good can you be with great defense and a weak block? Internationally, such teams can be pretty good these days. Look at Brazil. Not a strong blocking team, it finished fourth in the 1986 World Championships, thanks to great team defense and a very good offensive plan. To be the best, however, you have to coordinate your block and your defense, and you can't allow the two to become grossly disparate in skill level or in coordination. How do you do this?

To start with, you have to face reality. No block in the world will stop more than 20 to 30 percent of the attacks aimed at it. Your defense has to be prepared to receive a majority of the attacks. And quite a few of these might not arrive on a straight path, because the big goal of every block is to touch as many balls as possible. This makes the defense's job more difficult. Not only does your team have to line up straight on with the hitter, but you have to ready yourselves for the ball to come from a variety of strange trajectories. And the ball can arrive at widely varying speeds. For a baseball player, it would be like trying to hit a Nolan Ryan fastfall that turned into a Charlie Hough knuckle-ball 20 feet from the plate.

So be ready: no matter which direction the ball is going at first, you've got to expect it to come at you every single time. You can't let yourself get lazy. Any player can tell you what will happen if you relax. The very next hit will come into your area, and present you with an easy opportunity for a crucial save—but you won't be ready, and it could cost your team dearly. There's nothing worse than wishing that you had another chance at a play because you weren't ready the first time. Don't ever expose yourself to the possibility of being caught off guard.

Your team should know each of the opposing hitters' tendencies. If a player likes to hit the line, both the blockers and the defensive players should be aware of this preference. What you'd like to do is always take away the hitter's favorite shot or two by blocking those areas, and let the defenders handle the rest. Why? Because the hitter's favorite shot has to be his best, most reliable one. It is easier to block a hitter's best shot than it is to dig it—it will usually be coming at you so fast that you won't have time to react. If you block the best shot, then your diggers will be able to prepare themselves for the hitter's other shots, which will be less powerfully directed and easier to control.

Even if the hitter opts for his least favorite shot, it will be tougher to dig if it's deflected, because that requires a split-second adjustment by the defender. This is another reason why the blockers should take away only the hitter's favorite shot or two—that way, they'll be out of the way of the digger on the easier shots. If the opposing spiker likes to hit the angle, have the middle blocker take that shot. If his second choice is to hit down the line, take that with the end blocker. The blockers leave a nice, clear seam open—where the middle defensive player can control the shot.

The defenders' starting positions should be as follows. The left and right side diggers should be very shallow in the court. They must prepare to dig the quick attack, since the quick-hitter is usually the first option for the other team's offense. Quick-hitters very often have a middle blocker standing right in front of them, taking away any hits down the middle of the court. So they are left with hitting steep angles toward either sideline. Also, when opposing setters are in the frontrow, they will sometimes attack on the second hit by throwing the ball down with their left hand steeply to either sideline. The left and right diggers should be ready for both of those attacks.

Middle-back players have to make some choices. How do you decide where to stand? Because quick-hitters rarely attack straight down the middle of the court, I tried to use an educated guess as to which side I should lean toward. I didn't want to be standing exactly in the middle of the court. Most of the time, middle diggers will take a step to their left, as most quick-hitters like to hit directly in front of their right shoulder instead of cutting the ball back over their left shoulder (hitting an angle spike while facing in the opposite direction). But again, this depends on each particular hitter, and each defensive player should be aware of the hitters' individual tendencies.

This is what we called the starting team defensive formation (fig. 41). As the offensive play develops, these positions have got

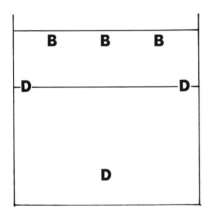

Figure 41. Defensive starting positions.
B = blocker
D = defender

to be adjusted because of the different preferences of the opposing hitters. If the set goes to the middle of the court (an X-set perhaps), the diggers won't need to change their position much, if at all. But if the set goes to either sideline, the digger down that line has to take a couple of steps back (fig. 42). When a hitter attacks from the outside, he or she must hit the ball with a flatter trajectory, because there is a much stronger block when the set goes high. If the side digger stays shallow, all the balls will come right

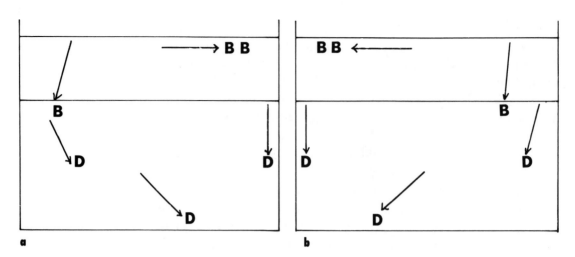

Figure 42. **Defense adjusting to a high set to a) the right and b) the left.**

at his or her head. You're better off making the ball arrive below your waistline.

Although the line digger has to back up to play the ball, he or she can't back up too far. Normally, the line digger is also responsible for any off-speed shots or tips (dinks) that come slowly over the blockers' outstretched arms. If your line digger is too slow to be able to move back and then recover forward for the tip shots, then your team has to make an adjustment. What we did, and what many other teams do, was to have our biggest, slowest players dig in the left back. Then all they had to do was take a step into the court when the ball came to their side. This is because they were in their proper starting position, straddling the 10-foot line. These guys often play a tip overhand because they are in such a great position behind the block for the short balls. As a hitter, I found it demoralizing when the slowest guy on the other team took my tip overhand.

Whenever one player moves to cover an area, another is opened up. So when a team has one player up short for the tips, the middle-back digger has to step over and cover behind, down the line. Then there is a hole in the deep middle, which the angle digger comes over to fill. It's like falling dominoes. That's what makes our game so great—the whole court can never be covered all at once. It's a matter of taking away what the hitter likes best with the block, and hoping to come up with his or her other shots with the diggers.

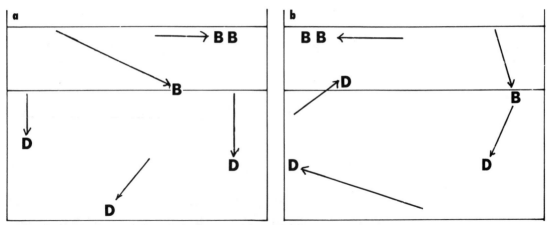

Figure 43. Tip coverage: a) the "blue" defense reacting to a high set to the right and b) the rotation defense reacting to a high set to the left. Note: the front-row player *away from* the set becomes a defender.

B = blockers
D = defenders

There are several ways to adjust if a team is having trouble picking up tip shots. One is what we called a "blue defense," where the off-blocker from the left side runs underneath the block to dig soft shots (fig. 43a). In the "rotation defense," as discussed above, the left-back player stays up to get short shots on the left side (fig. 43b). Both of these defenses can be reversed, depending on a team's personnel: that is, if you want to cover tips on the right with the right back, use a rotation instead of bringing the left-side off-blocker across.

When the set goes high to one side, the opposite-side blocker can back up and become a fourth digger. This off-blocker should get back to at least the 10-foot line, if not a step past it. By getting that far back, he or she frees the backcourt digger on that side to take a couple of steps backward. When the off-blocker covers the sharp angle, the deep-side digger can cover the corner.

Ideally, the blockers and diggers could set up a play before each point attempt. Something like, "We'll block number 15's line, number 3's line, and we'll take the straightaway shot on the quick-hitter, number 7." Some teams do this almost every play, but it demands extra communication. What the diggers should know is at least what blocking scheme has been called: read, stack, or whatever else the blockers have in their game plan.

There is another aspect of defense that teams often completely neglect, and that is team coverage. When a hitter goes to attack the ball, his five teammates should all gather around, expecting the ball to come back off the block. The Japanese team is superb at this; even though Japanese hitters get blocked often, the team will pick up the ball and the hitters will get two or three more chances to put the ball away. Now, who can't spike a ball to the floor with four chances and the knowledge that, no matter how hard the ball comes back, your team will usually keep it in play?

The setter and the backrow players are the most important in coverage formations because often the other hitters don't have time to get all the way under (fig. 44). The players, if possible, should form two rings of protection around the hitter as he goes to attack. The players should crouch very low, to give themselves more time to play the ball if it comes back hard, or even if it doesn't. And the first line of coverage should not stand directly underneath the hitter—they stand a couple of feet away so that they take more space.

If the block comes back, just be ready—expect the ball, so that you can make it go up in the air for the setter to get to. And if the set is very close to the net, definitely expect the ball to return because good hitters will tap the ball softly into the block so the coverage can make another whole play out of a set that's difficult to handle.

S = setter
Q = quick hitter
H = hitter
OH = off hitter
P = back-court passers

Figure 44. Hitter coverage: a) left side; b) right side.

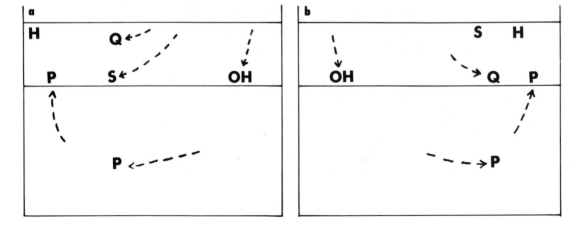

One way to practice coverage is to have four blockers stand on tables, reaching as far as they can over the net, trying to block—two blockers on the left and two on the right. Then have a hitter on the opposite side of the net hit outside sets (front and back)—some hard, some more softly—into the blocks. (The hitters should *try* to get blocked by the players on the tables.) The other five players on the hitter's team have to get 10 balls up before they rotate—and the hitting team has to cover 10 balls from each of the six turns of their rotation to complete the drill. (The blockers stay on their tables throughout.)

Team defense should be an exercise in coordination. The block should know what the defense is doing, the defense should know what the block is doing, and both should know the hitters' favorite shots. The whole purpose is for six players to blanket as much of the court as possible. The more times the block and the defense can touch the ball, the more scoring opportunities a team will have.

11

STRENGTH AND CONDITIONING

You alone control strength and conditioning: you don't have to depend on getting a good set, scouting another team, or finding enough players for a practice game. You can improve as a volleyball player, on your own, without needing other players, a court, a net, or even a volleyball.

Even a team with the six greatest players in the world won't win consistently, let alone every time, if it isn't strong and well conditioned. At the end of a match you should have to worry about what to do, not whether you're strong enough to do it. So be prepared: Fortify yourself.

On the USA team we practiced three to four hours a day, five days a week. We also worked out after practice each day, except before major competitions when we wanted all of our players to be healthy and fresh. We lifted weights in the evenings, four days per week. If we needed to work harder, we increased the intensity rather than the length of our practices. For about 11 months out of the year, we spent more time in one day training than any one match could last, ensuring our success through overpreparation.

Sometimes, no matter what a player does, he can't prepare himself for the physical demands of competition. There are times when I play on the beach in Florida or Brazil when my heart will be pounding at 150 beats per minute just from standing in the sun. It gets so hot that my vision blurs and my mind wanders, and I'll have to take a cold shower or pour a garbage can full of ice over my head at a break to cool off—happy that I'm still alive. There's no way I could prepare for that kind of challenge, unless I could build a court in a steam room, turn the temperature up to 113 degrees, and practice there four hours a day.

Designing Your Own Program

Fortunately, nothing you do will ever be quite that intense, but you'll still want to be prepared for the demands that volleyball can put on you.

It's always best to consult professionals—your doctor, coach, trainer, or physical therapist—before starting an individualized workout program. If you're ready to try it on your own, start by analyzing what you need to work on. If you're reasonably well proportioned but out of condition, put a particular emphasis on interval and aerobic training, so that you develop a quicker recovery. If you feel particularly weak in some portion of your body, maybe your upper body, emphasize that part in your weight workouts. Almost all volleyball players want to increase their leaping ability, so use part or all of the jump-training program described below, after making sure that you have already brought your strength and conditioning up to at least above-average levels.

Always give yourself at least one day of rest from the part of the program you've performed. For example, after a day's jump-training, give your legs at least a full day off. During that time you can lift weights with your upper body, but you should lay off anything that uses your legs. Give those muscles some time to recover—this will help you build your fitness in that part of the body more rapidly.

Use moderation. If you feel pain other than the normal burning of muscle fatigue, *stop.* If you are just starting to work out after a layoff period, don't kill yourself with a midseason training session. Take your time working yourself back into shape. And remember that each person has a different anatomical makeup and different tolerances to pain and exercise. Be flexible—and be sensitive to your body's needs and capacities while improving yourself physically. Your goal is to become the best volleyball player that you can—and each person has his or her own way of achieving that.

The National Team Program

With that advice in mind, I'd like to give you a brief introduction to the training program that we used during the years I was with the US national team. As you'll see, it is a complete program that builds all of the physical capabilities that a volleyball player needs. Keep in mind that this program was designed to challenge top-flight athletes. You'll have to adapt it to match your own level of fitness and your own conditioning needs. Still, it should give you some good ideas for setting up a well-rounded fitness program of your own.

Practice Makes Perfect

We always started practice with slow jogging and a lot of stretching. The stretching readies your muscles for the hardships of the next few hours. And more importantly, stretching keeps you healthier. Flexibility functions just as well as strength in allowing your body to absorb more stress and strain without injury. You really can't stretch too much—some of our players used to stretch three or four times a day.

After seeing the same gym so often for so long, players don't often come in excited about putting in another day on the hardwood. One thing we had in common, though, was an intense desire to compete and win. Our coach used this to his advantage by setting up competitions for us to finish our warm-ups. Games such as one-person tag, soccer, basketball, or warball are all good anaerobic workouts.

Sometimes we divided into teams for relay races: sprinting with a ball, sprinting without a ball, setting or bumping a ball to ourselves, dribbling, and running backward were just a few of the "events." The losers were punished with push-ups or sit-ups. Our program wasn't wealthy enough to offer rewards as incentives, so punishment was standard fare. Many of us did the push-ups and sit-ups, win or lose, but it feels better to choose to do them on your own (after winning the drill) than to be forced to do them (after losing the drill).

After these exercises, we might finish the warm-up with a game of three-man deep-court (behind the 10-foot line) volleyball. Or we might go through another good conditioner, a drill we called "coach-on-one": the coach would take one or two players at a time and have them chase down balls anywhere within the confines of the gym. And that meant anywhere. The coach usually mixed in a few hard-driven balls, with many thrown far enough away from the player that he had to dive for them. This drill could last from one to five minutes per group, depending on the coach's mood and the condition of the players. We dreaded the drill and sometimes felt like going "all-on-coach" afterward, but we could feel the positive effects on our fitness.

During practice, the conditioning takes care of itself, even in team drills where all 12 players are involved. For instance, we did a drill where the offense had to win one sideout (off serve reception) and put away six free balls, all in a row, against a full defense. The offense had to complete this six times, once for each rotation, to succeed. The drill once took us two and a half hours to finish, with one rotation lasting 50 minutes before they got it right. The guys who had it worst were the middle blockers. They had to jump on every play, and they were the happiest to get this drill over.

Weight Training

Our USA team weightlifting program concentrated on the main muscle groups and their complementary groups (the muscles which oppose them). We worked on the quads and the hamstrings in the legs, the abdomen and the lower back, the chest and upper back, the shoulders, and the triceps and biceps in the arms. This strategy followed the basic theory that if you ignore strengthening opposing muscle groups, you create imbalances where the stronger groups can literally tear or otherwise injure the weak groups. I based my own program away from my legs a little because of all the leg work I did in the gym, at the beach, while jump-training, and while running.

The best testimonial that I've seen to the value of a weight-lifting program is the case of Steve Timmons. In 1983, he was the 13th man on the squad, perilously close to being cut. He stuck with it and got strong enough physically to become one of the most dominant players in the world, especially at hitting from the backrow. "Big Red" got close to 300 pounds on the bench press and 100 miles per hour on the radar gun.

I've heard many different arguments about which exercises are best, whether to use free weights or machines, and how many sets and repetitions to perform. I don't think there is only one correct program for the sport of volleyball. One of the keys is to be flexible. Each person will need to strengthen different parts of his or her own body. The other key is to remember that doing something is almost always better than doing nothing, and that more is better—within reasonable limits. Don't hesitate to get into the weight room just because you're embarrassed to get started, or because you think you'll get sore. Getting sore is a great way to keep you going back—you won't get as sore if you keep at it.

You should always lift with a partner for safety, and for the extra motivation of having one of your peers around. We all have difficulty giving a maximum effort every time out, and having a partner there can make a big difference.

I prefer free weights because they offer you an endless variety of motion. If your shoulder hurts when you're using a machine, then you can't really use it effectively. If your shoulder hurts while you're lifting a free weight, you can try to adjust the angle of your lift a little so the pain disappears. That way you can always exercise the muscle groups you want to strengthen.

Start with the bigger groups before working the smaller ones. You might have trouble if you were to try bench-pressing after you had worked your triceps to exhaustion. My typical workout might go as follows:

1 · 3 sets of knee extensions
2 · 3 sets of hamstring curls
3 · 3 or 4 sets of bench presses
4 · 3 sets of incline presses

5 · 3 sets of bent rowing for the upper back
6 · 2 or 3 sets of abdominal curls
7 · 3 sets of back hyperextensions
8 · 3 sets of military presses
9 · 3 sets of tricep extensions with a dumbbell
10 · 3 sets of bicep curls

You can see the emphasis here—I want to build and maintain strength for spiking and blocking. The power in a spike comes from the abdominal snap (and sideways torque), from chest strength, and from the triceps. Blocking also demands strong abdominal muscles. I also do a lot of Olympic-style lifts—cleans, clean-and-jerks, snatches, push presses, etc.—because these demand and generate more power than any other resistance exercises, and power (strength *plus* speed) is exactly what you need on the volleyball court to jump high and move explosively. Find an experienced coach to teach you the proper techniques for these movements.

To maximize your development of power, you need the right combination of nutrition, rest, resistance training, and increase in your catabolic drive to build muscle mass. Read more about this in Colgan's *Optimum Sports Nutrition.*

Conditioning

Our conditioning program, which we performed on the days that we didn't jump-train, was an interval program (wind sprints, basically) with a steady progression toward shorter distances. Our aim was to get our heart rates up to 170 to 180 beats per minute by the end of each set, then take a rest to get it back down to about 100. The sign of being in good condition is *not* having a low resting heart rate—a fallacy many people believe. You're in good condition when your body can recover very quickly and make the heart rate drop back rapidly after raising it.

When you work on raising your heart rate—make sure that you do it *safely.* The level of heart rate that we worked toward is safe for Olympic athletes, but definitely *not* for recreational players. Check with your doctor to determine the right target rate for you.

We started each season with two-mile runs. As the season progressed, we went to sets of 440-yard dashes, then to 330s, 220s, and so on, until we approached the biggest competition of the year doing sets of 30-yard sprints. For example, on a day in the middle of the season we ran eight 220s: two at 85 percent (33 seconds), two at 90 percent (32 seconds), two at 95 percent (31 seconds), and two at 100 percent (30 seconds). Later on in the season we'd be running 55-yard sprints: two at 70 percent, two at 80 percent, two at 90 percent, two at 100 percent; then we would repeat the series.

The program was designed to start by building a good aerobic foundation, so that we could last through the long matches. Then the shorter sprints gave us the anaerobic capacity we needed to be strong through each of the hundreds of rallies we play in every match. And if we ever did get out of breath, we would be able to recover faster than the other team.

Jump-Training

Our jump-training program was based on plyometric theory. This theory states that while absolute strength is important in sports performance, power and explosiveness are even more critical. In fact, athletes usually don't have enough time to use their maximal strength capability. For example, when a volleyball player jumps off the ground after an approach he is not in contact with the ground long enough to generate a big voluntary force. The training depends on the fact that when a muscle is stretched before contracting, the contraction is faster and more forceful. The contraction also becomes more of a reaction, involuntary, so you don't need to think about making your muscle contract—it just does.

To train for power and explosiveness, we load the leg muscles and build up tension (like compressing a spring) and then contract them, releasing the force (like releasing a spring). This happens when you step off a bench, land on the ground with your knees flexed, and immediately jump back up as high as you can. The muscle force generated in this kind of exercise can be 10 to 20 times your body weight, yet you don't endanger yourself with the incredible amount of weight that you'd need to put on your shoulders to reproduce this force in the weight room.

Make sure you put yourself through a comprehensive strength and conditioning program before attempting jump-training. This prepares your body for the more strenuous activities of a program like the one below.

Two or three days a week, we began our jump-training right after the last drill in practice, which, studies now show, is the worst time to do plyometrics. You should perform them when your muscles are fresh, not fatigued. Anyway, the scheme was set up so that we had a number of stations to rotate through, with two to four players at each station. (Three players per station seems optimal, because each player gets to rest for twice the time that he exercises—just enough time to recover.) Following are some of the stations we used over the years.

At the "Russian leaper" station, the player wears a belt with two loops on the sides through which surgical tubing runs. The tubes clip onto a small platform with a padded carpet surface. Each time the player jumps, he gets pulled right back down by the big rubber bands. This is much easier than the other stations on the ankles, knees, and back because the player descends from a lower height. Do two to five sets of 20 to 45 repetitions. Some of the sets should be made up of a series of quick jumps, more like hops, without much knee bend or squat. Do these as fast as you can, jumping only a few inches off the ground, to practice speed. Other sets should be done with a maximum jump each time, landing with the knees flexed and exploding back up.

The station we called the "jump-box" (fig. 46) is a more difficult one. It's actually two boxes in one, with holes bored through the inner box to fit two dowels. The outside box rests solely on the two dowels to add some instability to the setup. The player jumps up onto the box, regains his balance without taking any steps, jumps off the box on the other side, lands softly, and then turns around and repeats. Do three sets of 10 to 20 repetitions. The top of the outer box usually sits at a height of 36 to 42 inches. We put the whole apparatus on gym mats so we didn't have to land roughly on a wood floor.

At the "step-ups" station, a bench is set in front of a player at a height of about 20 inches. With his right leg on the bench and his left leg on the floor, he jumps as high as he can off the right leg, switches legs in midair while crossing the bench, and lands with the left leg on the bench and the right leg on the floor. The

Figure 45. We used the "Russian leaper" to build leg strength and jumping ability.

player just goes up and down, up and down, switching legs each time, for three sets of 10 to 20 repetitions.

We always included a fourth station to see how high we were jumping, measuring our vertical leap against the antenna on a series of normal spike-jump approaches. That way we could track our improvement (or at least our lack of decline) over time.

Here are some variations or additions that you might want to try:

1. Wear a 13-pound weight belt, while doing block trips or approach jumps. Do these at a volleyball net to be sure that you can orient yourself correctly.

2. String up an elastic band for yourself at knee height and see how many times you can jump back and forth over it (side to side) in 30 seconds—without counting jumps where you touch the elastic. Then put it at waist height and do the same thing.

3. Line up a group of six or seven chairs in a row. Leapfrog one by one over the chairs, using a two-footed takeoff and landing. Make sure that you don't get tired on this one—you could lose both your shins if you catch them on the edge of one of the chairs. A better way to accomplish the same thing might be to jump over a piece of elastic stretched between six or seven players set up in a zigzag pattern (fig. 47), with the elastic at knee or waist level. Concentrate on jumping back as soon as you touch the ground.

4. Set up a station with car inner tubes filled with sand so that they weigh 50 to 75 pounds apiece. Each player wears one over his shoulders while doing maximum squat jumps. Make sure to explode back up as soon as you contact the ground instead of landing, squatting, pausing, and jumping. *Don't* try this exercise unless you are in great physical shape, or if you have a bad back or knees. It can put an enormous strain on the body.

Early in the season we might do two sets of 30 repetitions at each of the four basic stations. The most I can remember doing is five sets of 45 repetitions at six different stations—not one of my fonder volleyball memories. Make sure you take at least one day's rest for each day of exercise. Otherwise, you'll drive yourself into the ground, or hurt yourself.

Now that I play beach volleyball exclusively, I use only the jump-training exercises that can be performed in the soft sand. That means doing sets of 25 block or approach jump-sets. I work up to 14 sets of 25 before the season starts, then I don't do as

Figure 46. The jump-box.

The dowel holes are set close together so
that the outer box can rock back and
forth.

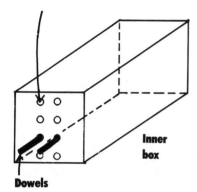

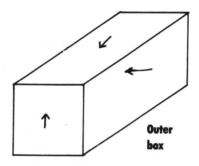

Inner box

Dowels

There are several sets of dowel holes so
that the box height can be adjusted.

The outer box is padded on the top and
on the edges.

Outer box

Jump on, jump off, then turn and
repeat.

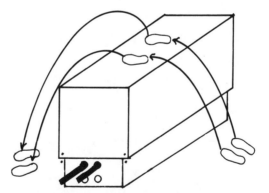

The outer box goes on top of the inner
box—again, the outer box rocks to make
the jumper work on balance.

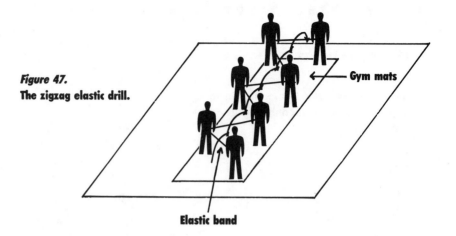

Figure 47.
The zigzag elastic drill.

Gym mats

Elastic band

many during the season because we have to jump so much during tournaments. The soft sand allows me to push my legs to exhaustion without pounding the rest of my body. And you may feel the added sensation, one that I used to feel, of moving much faster when you return to the gym.

I try not to do all of these workouts all of the time. My mind tells me, "You can always do something more, something extra to help you play better." Meanwhile, my body says, "If you listen to your mind, I'm going to turn into Jell-O and I'll never play again." We all have to tread a fine line, building strength and conditioning while staying healthy and not tearing our bodies apart.

12
COACHES AND TEAMMATES

Our country's lust for athletics generates so much publicity that players' and coaches' images often get blown completely out of proportion. The images we have of Woody Hayes tearing down yard markers and punching opposing players, of Vince Lombardi teaching his players that "Winning isn't everything, it's the only thing," and of Bobby Knight tossing a chair onto a basketball court can confuse our sense of what role a coach should really play.

Players get exposed to many different coaching styles as we work our way up through a variety of styles and levels of volleyball training and develop into mature (or should I say older?) players. We each have our own expectations of coaches and coaching, but I'd like to give you some idea (even though I'll have to make a few generalizations) of what players on the US national team preferred. This will help you understand that team better, and will give some coaches a better feel for what goes through the minds of their players.

What is a coach? I think of a coach as the leader, the person who designs the team's system, and the person toward whom players look for guidance in running that system. The coach has to assess the talent he or she has available, put together a system that best utilizes that talent, and then let things flow during the competition. By the time the game starts, the system, if well designed, should operate smoothly on its own momentum. (Players will obviously need more guidance if the system fails than if it succeeds.)

Our players looked at a coach, then, as a leader, as an expert in the sport, and as our friend. The coaching style we liked best was one that respected the players as human beings and as friends. Most players feel a strong need for the coach to like them and to be positive with them, just as any other friend might. Although I didn't need much positive or negative response, I know I wanted the coach to like me. But not all coaches feel as if they need to be liked or accepted by their players.

The players on the USA team all agreed that a coach should set out his or her rules very clearly, so that there's no confusion among the players. This goes for coaches who have many rules as well as for those who have very few. Most of the coaches I've played for have used very few rules. If you are a coach who likes to have considerable control over your players' lives outside of volleyball, it will help those players understand your demands if you give them a reason for each rule that you set up—like curfews, for example.

If you like to be more flexible in your approach, make sure to explain to your players that you think they are such responsible athletes that they should know how to take care of their bodies and prepare for games themselves. If they abuse the privilege of being treated like adults, you can always come down a little harder on them until they shape up. (It took me a while to learn how to take care of myself. In my early days on the national team, some of us would stay out until all hours of the night, and act very irresponsibly.)

Whatever style you choose, flexible or otherwise, make sure to spell out all of your guidelines very clearly. That way none of the players can try to interpret the rules in his or her favor if a disagreement arises.

We also preferred that a coach be consistent in his meting out of punishment or praise. Let's say that a coach lets three players arrive 10 minutes late to practice without any retribution. What will the players think if he forces a punishment drill on another player who arrives a minute late the next day? They might think that the coach hates that player, or that he considers the other three special, or both. They might even think that it is all right to arrive 10 minutes late, but not 1 minute late. Or they might think that it is acceptable to be late on a Tuesday, but not on a Wednesday. None of those conclusions can benefit the team. So whatever rules or guidelines the coaches set up and use, they should abide by them as consistently as possible. Otherwise, the players might get so confused about what is good or bad behavior that they lose sight of their top priorities.

One of a coach's most important abilities is to adapt his coaching style to the players he has. When I first started playing on the national team in 1981, Doug Beal was the coach. We had a lot of young players join the team—players who showed the potential to be great. It took a lot of work to improve from 19th in the world to 1st over a three-year period. We needed to be pushed beyond our limits, so we could learn how great our potential was. Thanks to Doug's pushing, our limits were much higher at the LA Olympics than they had been in 1981. I can't say that I enjoyed it all of the time, and I can say that I hated it some of the time. No matter how much we disliked it, Doug made us do what we had to do to accomplish our goal, which was to win a medal at that Olympics. He knew what it would take to develop our raw talents. He adapted his methods to our team—and it worked.

After 1984, however, those of us who remained from the LA Olympics probably couldn't have taken the continued discipline and drudgery. We already knew how to win, and we were veterans of pressure-filled, monumentally important matches. We were the veterans of some disasters, too. After all we'd been through, we didn't need the "little boy" treatment; we needed to be respected more, and treated like the adults we were. Marv Dunphy, who took over for Beal in 1985, understood the situation and coached accordingly. He was able to learn from us as well as implement his own ideas. He maintained the control all coaches need to be successful, but he stayed flexible in dealing with his more experienced players.

Coaches play a critical role in running team practices. We liked it best when our coach established a steady rhythm with his practice schedule. We preferred to begin and end practices at the same times every day, and to start every practice with the same basic warm-up pattern. We'd start with some running to raise our body temperature, followed by a rigorous stretching routine. As a final warm-up, we liked a little variety: perhaps more running, some competitive setting drills, little games of tag, relays, or other games such as basketball.

Yes, I sound inconsistent. We wanted practice to have the same structure every day, but we also preferred that the drills vary from one day to the next. We also liked the tempo of practice to follow the same pattern day after day. The coach could make it very tough on our bodies by not arranging the drills in the proper order. If he ran his hardest drill early in the practice, then ran an easy drill that let us cool down, and then another difficult drill, we found our bodies riding through a roller-coaster—getting very warm, cooling off, warming up again, etc. This reduced our stamina and made us more prone to injury. We would rather have the workload rising on a steady course until we reached the most difficult exercise near the end of practice. We'd end with an easy drill to cool down, then stretch to keep our muscles loose for the next day.

Coaches should make sure to keep practices in sync with their overall goals for the season. If, as a coach, you want to see improved blocking from your team, you should emphasize blocking in many of the practices. If the biggest matches are at the end of the season (which they almost always are), then the hardest practices and conditioning should come early in the season. You should be able to hold back a little on workouts near the end, so that the players are healthy and fresh for those big matches. One thing you don't want to do is to work your players so hard that they are too tired or too sore or just plain too burnt out on volleyball to perform well at the end of the season.

When you are setting the lineups, you'll have some difficult decisions to make. You can't possibly keep all twelve players happy. But you'll have more to worry about if the six players who don't start aren't upset. If they aren't, then they don't crave being out on the court enough, or they just don't care at all. Normally, players should be begging to play.

Encourage your players to be students of the game—to think about the why and how of techniques and strategies. Even if most of their ideas turn out to be impractical, your players will at least better understand what you, as a coach, are trying to accomplish. And who knows, they may think of some new variations for the offense you've installed, or think of a new way to neutralize a particularly effective hitter.

Along those lines, you can help your players tremendously by sitting down with them to set out team and personal goals. That way, the players have something to shoot for every day, something to focus their energy on. You can get goals for how many wins and how few losses you would like to end up with after the season, or for what place you'd like to finish in. Your team should have some input in the setting of these goals.

If you keep statistics on your team's performance, you can also establish goals for how they should perform in each match, in different parts of the season, and over the season as a whole. It helps players to set goals for individual improvement in specific parts of their games over the course of a season. I tried to do this with my serve. We kept track of my serving statistics—and I did improve, by 20 percent. Always try to use quantitative measures of a player's progress, so that he can get a clear picture of how his game is developing.

One thing I've really appreciated in all of the coaches that I've played for has been their honesty. Being treated with honesty and integrity means a great deal to me. If I am doing something wrong, I want to know about it as soon as possible, so that I won't develop bad habits. And I respect a coach more when he or she can tell me straightforwardly what skills or attitudes I am deficient in.

It is very important to be open with players when you're conducting tryouts. If you have to cut players, tell them why, and give them some advice as to which skills they need to improve, and how they might go about becoming the type of player you would like to have on your team. Getting cut from a team isn't an easy situation for anyone. You can make it much easier by being honest and positive.

Still, none of us wants a coach to crow about our mistakes, to try to embarrass us into playing better. The power game that some coaches play, screaming at their players, is a waste of energy. The coach is supposed to work *with* the team, not *against* it. Nobody needs to be mentally abused. We're all human beings, right? I can understand coaches getting upset if their players keep making the same mental errors over and over again, but they shouldn't go overboard in response. Players may feel so besieged with threats and embarrassments that they feel they are competing in spite of their coach. A team is at a real disadvantage if the players feel that their coach isn't doing everything possible to assist them in competing.

It's much more effective for a coach to try to keep an even temperament at all times. That way, when the coach does raise his voice just a little bit, the players realize that something is gravely wrong. Getting upset with players on rare occasions is going to have a much greater impact on them than ranting and raving every day.

It's also important for coaches to stay calm during a game. We liked to have our coach at least act like he knew what he was doing. Panic in a coach translates to chaos on the court. Convince your players that you are poised, and they will play with poise. A coach should also make sure to keep his more emotional players (like me) under just enough control that they don't hurt their team out on the court. Our team was at its best when we played with emotion, but we sometimes carried that to an extreme—getting upset with the referee's calls, with the other team, and with each other.

Many people remember our flare-up with Brazil during the semifinals of the Seoul Olympics. We would never initiate taunting or yelling under the net, but Bill Neville taught us never to back down if the opposition was trying to intimidate us. After handling the Brazilians during most of the match, we got sick of their screaming and started screaming right back. They got us so fired up that we finished out the match quickly. Our coach needed to keep just enough rein on that intense emotion that we could still play at our best.

I like a coach who will say something constructive during time-outs. Marv Dunphy and Al Scates were particularly good at looking at the positive side of a situation where things weren't working for us. Instead of criticizing our poor play, they would encourage us, saying something like, "All right, here's the play we will run to get a sideout—then we're going to do this [tactical plan] to help us win the next point, start to play better, and win this game and match." Talk to your team positively—infect the players with your confidence in them.

After the match, win or lose, a coach can make a big difference in how the players feel. If they have just suffered a terrible loss, the coach can point out how they lost, and more importantly, how the team can learn from its mistakes and what the players can do to change the outcome the next time they play. Emphasize learning from bad experiences—we would never have become such a great team without living through some horrendous losses. We learned about perseverance from the Japanese more than once. Once we were ahead of them 14–3 in the fifth game and ended up losing 16–14. We used the memory of that experience to persevere through some of the difficult matches that followed.

You can also help your players put a big win in perspective. Unless it's the last game of the season, you should caution them against getting too excited, because there are always more matches to play. Remind your players to be a little more humble and a little more classy, win or lose, so that each player can take pride in being a member of the team.

Those are just a few of my thoughts on how to maintain a great relationship of mutual respect between coaches and players. Coaches have big responsibilities—it's not easy to be honest, fair, a good leader, a goal setter, a motivator, and a teacher.

13

BEACH
VOLLEYBALL

I've been asked a lot of questions in my career, the two most common ones being: "Which do you like better, beach volleyball or indoor volleyball?" and "What's the difference between the beach and indoors?"

I'll answer the latter below, but as for the former: although I love both games, if I had to choose one for the long term, I'd opt for the beach. And that's what I did when I retired in July 1989 from the USA team: I had overloaded on travel time and gym time. There's nothing like playing a few outdoor games on a beautiful day, and, unfortunately, I have to do that now that I'm a full-time beach player. Also, because the softer surface is easier on your body, you can play on the sand for the rest of your life.

I liked playing indoors for many reasons, the best being that it's an Olympic sport. When you win a World Championship or an Olympic gold medal, you've reached the pinnacle, and I coveted the sense of absoluteness, of knowing we were the best team on the planet.

I also like beach volleyball for many reasons. The beach itself is usually reason enough, because it's a great place to be, but it's the sport I grew up with and a game I'll never give up. Although there's less protocol and a more relaxed atmosphere for the fans, it's just as intense, since the stakes (international championships and prize money) keep rising. A player can control more of his own destiny with just one teammate, rather than five, on the court. The beach game satisfies a player's ego more and great plays are easier for fans to notice and appreciate. And now beach volleyball will achieve the same prestige as the indoor game with its inclusion in the 1996 Summer Olympics in Atlanta.

What most appeals to me, though, is how well playing doubles on the beach forces you to learn each skill. You can't specialize in being just a great hitter or a great setter. The beach is the perfect spawning ground for all-around players because you've got to master *each* technique: passing, setting, hitting, blocking, digging, and serving. I learned volleyball at the beach, and I would have been a weaker indoor player without that training.

You might ask, "How do two players cover the same area that six do indoors?" The two players have no choice but to split the court right down the middle—one's got the left side and the other will take the right side. Players concentrate on playing a particular side because it's very difficult to play one side well when you are constantly changing back and forth. It's the same as when a player has trouble switching frequently between beach and indoors: the jack-of-all-trades problem. For instance, Sinjin Smith, the all-time leader in tournament wins, has played almost exclusively on the right side and been a better player for it. I've always been a left-side player. This is one of only two areas in which beach players can specialize. The other is on defense, which I'll cover later.

So why does the beach force an athlete to learn so much? Because if he has a weakness there's no hiding it. Since we almost always use all three contacts, the player who receives the serve *has* to, or, depending on how you look at it, *gets* to hit. For example, if my partner were a weak passer (or if he fatigues easily), other teams would serve him. If I were a weak setter I'd compound our problems. And if my partner were a poor hitter we'd have three strikes against us and he'd be calling me, or I'd be calling him, "future ex-partner" (a Pat Powers quote). That's often what players mean when they say there was "bad chemistry" between partners.

Passing

Remember the first strike I mentioned: a bad pass. I said in the indoor section that bad passing dooms a team to mediocrity. That's even more true in beach doubles because, with a strong wind or a blinding sun or both, it's difficult enough to set a *good* pass, but it's pure misery to set a lousy one. Speaking of the wind, one of the first principles you should learn is to keep everything low—with both passes and sets, the wind can and will inflict chaos on the ball. The longer it's in the air, the farther the wind will blow it.

The techniques of passing are similar to those discussed in the indoor bump chapter. One difference is your ready position: you need to be lower and better balanced in beach doubles because you have to be able to spring in any direction when passing tough jump-serves. The forearm and body position, the grip, concentration, and confidence factors are the same. Strive to center yourself on the ball just as you would indoors.

Your target for the pass differs also. Ideally, you should direct it straight in front of you about five feet from the net. You want to direct the pass straight ahead for two reasons: (1) your partner can anticipate where the pass will go and start running toward that spot as you pass the ball, and (2) passes that spray all over the court are more difficult to set accurately, but a straight-ahead pass makes it easier for your partner to set you in your favorite spot. This is true whether you play the left or right side, whether you're left- or right-handed. And you want to pass off the net because your partner doesn't have the luxury of waiting at the net for the pass like an indoor setter. Give him some room so he doesn't tangle himself in the net.

Setting

Setting is simple enough: set the ball cleanly and put it exactly where your partner wants it. Okay, it only sounds simple. In days past you had to face where you set the ball, side-sets were illegal. And you had to set the ball with no spin or risk the referee calling a mishandled ball, although indoor players have never had to worry about spin. Nowadays you can face any direction while setting, but you still have to take most of the spin off your sets. That's one of my gripes about American beach volleyball: the setting interpretation has been so strict that (1) players (including me) hold onto the ball too long, called "deep-dishing," so they can take the spin off the ball; (2) most of the other players resort to bump-setting. Aesthetically, it's more appealing to watch overhand setting because it's an art in and of itself. And how will we develop more good setters if everybody's afraid to set overhand? I favor loosening the rules still more, even if it takes some of the good setters' advantage away. Until that happens, take extra care when setting high digs.

Still, whenever possible you should set overhand. Overhand sets are more accurate and easier to time and to hit. The techniques of setting mirror those of indoors: same hand and body position, same stiff fingers and loose wrists.

There's one big difference on the beach. You don't need to deceive opponents because once your partner receives the serve, everyone on the beach knows who will hit the ball. So make it accurate; put the set only where your partner wants it, nowhere else. If he wants it high and outside, do it. If he wants it low and inside, do that.

I prefer a low set because it's easier for me to time, so I tell my partners that. Most players prefer the set off the net two or three feet because they almost always face a blocker. Don't be afraid to help the setter during the play. If you dig a ball off the court you could say, "Just put high in the middle," or, "Anywhere!" if it's a really poor dig. Sometimes you'll run to other areas of the court to dig so you might yell, "Set it on the right!" or, "Behind you!"

If you haven't yet developed confidence in your hand-setting, or your partner likes bump-sets better, learn to bump from behind the ball and face exactly where you want the ball to go. It's really hard to bump-set a ball accurately from thirty feet away even if you are facing the target, let alone when you aren't. Take the wind and the spin on the ball into consideration (whether you set with your hands or a bump) because both these factors greatly affect the flight of the set after it leaves your hands. If the wind is in your face, push the set a little harder. If the topspin on the ball is going away from you, don't push it quite so hard.

Hitting

Beach players spike over the same height net as indoors, which used to seem like no easy feat. Until about 1980 both defenders would stand back and dig, patiently waiting to make a great play or receive a free point on the other team's mistake. But hitters gradually grew bigger and stronger and teams ran out of patience scoring points so slowly. Blocking with one player while the other covered the rest of the court became the standard strategy, not just an occasional surprise tactic. In 1986 blocking over the net was legalized on the AVP Pro Beach Tour, further promoting the block as a way to score points quickly. Since the blocker can take away some of the harder shots, the spiker often places the ball softly into any one of the four corners. This is where beach technique differs most: hitters use soft shots that would never succeed indoors, and the rule on the beach prohibiting open-hand tips (dinks) compels you to learn precise control of these shots.

When hitting on the beach you should use modified versions of the techniques described in the indoor hitting chapter (chapter 3). Most players use the standard four-step approach: for a right-hander, that would be a step with your right foot, a power step off your left, plant your right foot on the ground, then your left, and then jump up to spike (reverse that for left-handers). And, just like indoors, if you're playing on the left side, you want to be facing the angle a bit (as a right-hander), to be able to hit the angle or turn your torso hard to the left to hit the line. On the right side (as a right-hander) you want to face the line, so you can hit the line or turn your torso hard to the left to hit the angle. Reverse those ideas if you're left-handed.

Unlike indoors, where you can begin your approach from the same distance off the net each time, your beach approach needs to be more flexible—you just start it from wherever you passed the serve. So if you get served deep, you might start your approach from the back line, and you may need six or eight steps instead of four to get to the net. Incidentally, you may have noticed a quirk in my approach. I changed to a goofy-footed four-step approach, only on the beach and only on the left, so I could hit the line more effectively. That is: left, right, left-right, opposite of the normal indoor approach I use. I don't recommend this for anyone else. You're always better off keeping things simple, so do as I say, not as I do.

Since you're not going to jump as high in the soft sand, you don't want to broad jump at all. Instead, you want to get every inch of your jump going upward, so approach to hit immediately after you pass, run toward the spot where you think your partner will set, and make last-second adjustments as the set descends. Of course, your timing on the beach will differ because the sand is so much softer and slower to move in that you have to begin your approach sooner. Remember, however, that there are all types of beach courts and the type of sand can greatly affect play. Soft, deep sand is obviously more difficult to move and jump in, while hard-packed sand can be similar to playing on grass. Try to practice on a court with the deepest sand possible, which will make you a much stronger hitter when you enter a tournament with a number of hard-packed courts to play on.

You don't have to be able to hit the ball straight down to be a good beach player. Instead, you have to master the four-corner offense: dink, cut, deep line, deep angle. I had to learn those shots early—my dad and I competed in tournaments for four years before I could even hit a ball downward. You need good shots, whether you're short or tall, to put the ball away off a bad set. And when a blocker is up (which is almost always the case on the Pro Tour), leaving so much of the court unprotected, you don't often have to swing hard. In fact, it's smarter and easier not to. Why not save energy and keep the opponents off guard by mixing it up a little?

Before discussing the various shots, here are two principles I urge you to heed: (1) Always, always hit the ball *into the court.* You don't have to make it roll along the net or bounce on the knot in the corner. As my coach at Santa Barbara High School, Rick Olmstead, used to say, "You could land a helicopter over there— hit the ball *in.*" (2) Always, always approach a hit hard. Begin every approach thinking "kill," because you can always change your mind and make a shot. If you saunter in, thinking "shot," you limit your options and you'll get stuffed or dug more easily.

Hit the ball with an open hand for better control of your shots. The wider you spread your fingers, the more surface area you'll have to make contact, which will give you more command of your shots and better spin on the ball.

Remember the clock from the hitting chapter—to hit the

ball straight ahead, strike it at twelve o'clock. To direct the ball to your right, strike it on the left side, around ten or eleven o'clock. And to direct the ball to your left, hit it to the right of center at one or two o'clock.

The key to making great shots is to use the same motion and energy until the last possible second every time you attack. As I said before, approach hard and jump hard every time. Contact the ball at the peak of your jump with a fully extended arm every time. And contact the ball above and a few inches in front of your head every time. That consistency makes you more deceptive and harder for your opponents to read.

To make a good dink, your arm swing should slow down at the last instant. Continue the arm swing and wrist snap in slow motion so that the ball travels upward and forward just enough to clear the net and fall on the other side, while still having some topspin. The topspin will help the ball fall away from the approaching defense, and will help it roll over the net in case you hit the tape. Remember that if there's a blocker, you'll have to make the shot higher (to clear his hands) and deeper (so he can't land, lunge backward, and pick up your dink).

I think the cut shot is the most difficult and the prettiest, because you have to make the ball cross the net up to five or ten feet away from you, and then fall short to avoid the defense. That's why you'll rarely get blocked making this shot—the ball crosses the net so far from the blocker when you've hit it right. I particularly enjoy watching cuts from right-handers on the right (or left-handers on the left)—watch Scott Ayakatubby, Adam Johnson, or Mike Dodd and you'll see cuts that are works of art.

To cut from the right side of the court, what part of the ball should you hit? That's right, hit the ball at around one or two o'clock, to make it go left. Some players even hit it at three o'clock for a really thin slice. Again, use your last-second, slow-motion arm swing and wrist snap to hit this off-speed shot. As you contact the ball, snap your wrist over and around the ball to make it go to the side. And if you're a right-hander, make sure you don't contact the ball over your left shoulder in an effort to make it go left—that's a common error. Instead, let your wrist do the work.

Cutting from the left, as a right-hander, is easier because you can reach a little outside your body line as you snap your wrist around the left side of the ball, at about ten o'clock.

The deep-line and deep-angle shots are more like normal

spikes because you get to take a little harder swing at the ball. Aim both shots about three feet in from the sideline *and* three feet in from the endline, in case the wind picks up or you misjudge your strength. Using your slow arm swing, make sure you put topspin on these shots to keep the ball inbounds. When hit well, the shot looks like what some people call it: a rainbow, landing softly deep in the court.

One common mistake players make on their deep-line shot is to hit around the ball (like a cut) too much so it sails sideways out of bounds. Hit it closer to twelve o'clock so it flies true.

The shot you see the least is the deep angle. Many players don't realize that you have over 40 percent more court there to hit toward, about 30 feet down the line vs. over 42 feet on the angle. That means you have more room behind the digger in which to land the ball, especially if he is leaning forward, or is cheating toward your deep line or your cut shot.

One advanced trick you might want to experiment with: some players look under the net as the pass goes toward the net, to help them see where the defender is and give themselves a better idea of where to place their shot in the open part of the court. Some even take a second look as the set ascends, then bring their eyes back to the ball as the set and the player meet in the air. For many players, even advanced competitors, taking their eyes off the ball after it has been set is a difficult trick to learn. In fact, the only players I've seen who can do it effectively are Kent Steffes, Adam Johnson, and Sinjin Smith. The rest of us may never master this skill, which means we have to rely on our partners to call out where the defender is (more on this technique later in this chapter).

Here's one way to practice your four-corner offense: set up targets in all four corners, or mark those areas with lines in the sand. Throwing the ball up to yourself, hit a set of ten or twenty balls softly into each area. Remember you don't have to be the most intimidating hitter to be the best—consistency wins out over muscle. You can add a defensive player on the other side of the net and tell him to move forward, backward, left, or right just before you hit so you can practice reacting correctly and hitting the soft shot to the area he just vacated. If there's a third player available, use him to set.

Then you can make the drill more competitive by having the defender really try to make a play on every ball. You can play a game: the hitter has to put fifteen soft shots down before the digger gets five to seven of them up.

Eventually players have to learn to hit around or over the block, so players should progress to hitting sets of ten or twenty balls against one blocker. Have him make exaggerated moves to the line or angle at first, and when you've gotten the hang of hitting where he's not, have the blocker try to stop you every time. You can vary this drill by competing: you hit ten against him, and he hits ten against you (or alternate, with the setter stepping back and forth under the net each time)—see who can block more. This is one I use a lot now because you only need three players.

Blocking

There are many reasons why you always see a blocker at the net on the Pro Tour. First, it's too easy to hit the ball without one (an open net is a rare and exciting treat for us). Second, as I mentioned before, the rules were changed in 1986 to allow blockers to penetrate the plane of the net. Third, since many of our events are on temporary "beaches" where the sand is more flat and compact, hitters can jump higher, allowing them to hammer the ball down even from far off the net. And fourth, because none of us (except Mike Dodd) can sit back and dig heat all day like Jim Menges or Ron Lange used to.

When I teach indoor blocking I tell people, "Have a really good ready position, watch the setter, move and watch the hitter, then jump and reach; your goal should be to touch every ball." But what about blocking on the beach?

With just two players, you don't need to read the setter—everyone on the beach knows that he can only set his partner. Besides, reading some of the bump-setters out there would be enough to make you dizzy, because even they don't know where the ball is going. You don't need to have great footwork—just go stand in front of the guy who received serve. And you certainly can't expect to touch every ball; half the time, the opposing hitter will just loop a rainbow shot over you that even Shaquille O'Neal couldn't touch.

The bigger you are or the higher you jump (or both) the more you want to try to take *everything* away from the hitter. Start by taking an area, but be ready to react and block a different shot at the last second.

One thing *is* the same whether you're blocking indoors or on the sand: your ready position. You should find a comfortable distance from the net (about 12 to 18 inches). Too close and you'll net, too far away and you won't be able to put your hands above and across the net when you jump. Your hands should be at about head height, your knees slightly bent, feet about shoulder-width apart.

Watch the set closely as it ascends: if it goes away from the net, you should back off to play defense because there's much less chance the hitter will swing hard.

Once the set starts falling, you *have* to look at the hitter. I know it's hard, but you've got to wrench your gaze away from the ball, mainly because it won't go anywhere without a hitter. Watching the hitter shows you his line of approach: some hitters like to swing in the direction of their approach, others prefer the opposite, so if you remember hitters' tendencies, you'll have a better chance to stuff them. And by watching the hitter, you'll see which direction he's facing (most hitters like to attack where they're facing) and which direction his arm swing goes. Approach line, body direction, and arm swing are your three main clues to read the hitter.

Next you need to jump and reach. Usually you'll jump a little after the hitter did, because you want to be up there when the ball crosses the net, not when the hitter contacts the ball. The farther the hitter is from the net, the later you'll jump. As you leave the ground, push your hands over and *across* the net and try to keep them over there as long as you can. It's critical that you penetrate the net plane to prevent any balls from falling between you and the net.

What dictates where the ball will go if you actually touch it? Your hand position, of course. If you face your hands up, that's where the ball will go; if you face them out of bounds, you'll probably block it at the referee, which you may have desired anyway, but it won't win the play. So point your palms downward toward the middle of your opponent's court to keep the ball in play, with your forearms and hands just wide enough to let an occasional ball through—you want to take the biggest continuous area possible. And for that same reason, spread your fingers as widely as you can.

Now let's talk about blocking within the context of a doubles team. If one player is clearly superior at blocking, or if one of you is clearly inferior on defense, then that player should do most of the blocking. When one player does most of the blocking, he's going to have to be fast (to follow his own serve and get to the net in time to block) and well conditioned (to block every play, all tournament long). If, on the other hand, the two of you are fairly equal at blocking and defense, you should think about sharing duties. If you do, whoever serves should play defense while the partner blocks. That's what I prefer, because my partner and I are free to focus on our jump-serving, and both of us stay fresh.

As I said before, the blocker should begin by taking an area: usually the line, the angle, or the middle. Try not to show the hitter what you're taking until the last second. The digger should usually start in the area left open: if the blocker takes line, the defender digs angle. The decision of what area to block is based mostly on taking away the opposing hitter's favorite shots. But good hitters adapt, so you shouldn't stick with your original strategy too long if it's ineffective.

Once you've decided what area you're going to block, you need to let your partner know. Most teams use signals, before the serve, like this: the blocker stands with his hand behind his back (one finger means line, two mean angle, fist for middle, etc). That call would apply to either of the opposing hitters, wherever the server goes. Or the blocker could make two calls, one for each hitter, by putting two hands behind his back. Some players even prefer to signal after the pass has been made to take into account what line of approach the hitter might be taking—this is what I prefer.

Blocking drills can be done with two players, but are much more affective with at least three; a hitter, a setter, and the blocker. With two players, one could toss balls to himself to hit while the other blocks. Practice blocking the line for a set of ten, then the angle, and then a set where the hitter mixes it up and the blocker has to try to anticipate where the ball will go.

With three players, you can start with the same drill but use a setter so the blocker gets more realistic practice. One of my favorites, which I described briefly in the hitting section above, is where two players alternate trying to block each other while the setter steps back and forth under the net. Play twenty balls (the hitter isn't allowed to make shots, only hard spikes) then rotate. Do three sets total. Each player blocks and hits on the right, and on the left, and also sets once. To make it competitive keep track of your total blocks or kills and see which player can accumulate the most.

Here's a good drill to practice keeping your eye on the hitter and not the ball: from behind the blocker's back a third player tosses sets over the net to the hitter. That way the blocker never gets to look at anything but the hitter, to watch for those clues I mentioned above. At first the hitter should try to get blocked every time, but work up to where he tries to avoid the block.

Digging

Defense is a lonely business. These days, we're almost always left to cover the whole court while our partners stand at the net and block. Can one player cover 90 percent of the court by himself *every* play? No. But a good defender *can* cover the court the majority of the time.

The most difficult thing about defense is to stay ready for both hard hits *and* soft shots. You know the hard hits will come only to your half of the court (assuming your partner can adequately block the other half), but the soft shots can go anywhere. Many players are good at one or the other: certain players dig in (also called putting "cement shoes" on) and control opposing hitters' best heat but can't move three feet to make a play. Other players move around the sand like a water spider on a lake, but send everything hit at them into bleachers. Your goal should be competence at both.

Attitude plays a role in good defense—the best defenders believe they can get their hands on every ball that gets by the blocker and that no ball is impossible to pick up.

And finally, you have to be able to anticipate where the hitter is going to direct the ball. Just as when you're blocking, approach line, body orientation, and arm swing will be your three main clues as to where the ball might go. Study opposing hitters to learn their favorite shots, what they do when approaching outside in, or inside out, and what they do when they're in trouble (with a bad set, for instance). There is no substitute for months or years of just playing—it takes a long time to develop that sense of knowing where the ball will go, and moving your-self there, that all the guys on the Pro Tour have.

Your starting position will normally be about ten to fifteen feet away from the net (depending on how steeply the opposing hitter spikes or how good a cut shot he has) and into the court enough to dig a typical angle shot. Spread your feet fairly wide apart, knees bent, back upright. This well-balanced position allows you to make quick, strong moves in any direction.

Your upper arms should hand down perpendicular to the ground, while your forearms will be parallel to the ground or even higher, since you'll have to dig more balls at chest or face level (remember that overhand digs are legal on the sand). Keep your forearms a foot or two apart without gripping your hands together—it's quicker when you only have to move one arm to meet the other to play a ball to the side.

It's almost too obvious to mention, but I'll say it anyway—watch the hitter as long as you can for clues to where the ball will go. Then, when the ball does arrive, play it with your fore-arms, both of them whenever possible, for control. I've seen too many games lost because a lazy player one-armed the ball and shanked it. If the ball is hit really hard you may have to pull your arms back a little to absorb some of the shock and control it better. I also use this technique when receiving jump-serves to give my partner a softer pass with less spin.

If the ball comes at your face, and it's hard-driven (it has to be for this open-hand dig to be legal), use the overhand dig. Start with your fingers spread wide. Then let the ball hit your palms and fingers all at once and push it straight up. The master at this dig is Scott Friederichsen—watch how he can take a ball, almost grab-bing it, and have it come out without sticking and without spin.

If the ball is hit away from you take a strong step toward it—don't give up on it. The sand is soft, so hurl your body after the ball and do everything you can to play it with two arms. If you can only get one arm on it, use the arm that's closest to the ball—don't use your right arm every time just because you're right-handed. And don't try to be perfect with the dig—just get it up high in the middle of the court where your partner can get to it. Then prepare to hit, but don't expect a perfect set—be ready to hit from anywhere.

One thing the beach game taught me was how to play the ball low, giving myself more time to react and make a better play. If your partner shanks one into the net, go under and sit down or kneel to wait for the ball to fall back out. Playing the ball low also applies to a form of defense much ignored on the beach: coverage. After you set your partner and call the right shot, get low and wait for a blocked ball to come at you. I saved a tournament in San Diego a few years ago when I stayed low and covered the ball after Kent got blocked on tournament point.

Mix up your strategy to keep your opponents guessing. If your partner blocks line you can: (1) stay in the angle; (2) fake going to the line, and come back to the angle; (3) run early to get the line shot; (4) run late to get the line shot; (5) run to get the line shot, then sprint back hoping to lure the hitter into a cut shot; (6) or you can even start digging behind the line blocker, then run to the angle at the last second. Reverse all that when your partner blocks angle. And I'm sure you can think of more.

You should adjust your strategy based on the opposing hitters' tendencies. For instance, if a hitter likes the soft line shot, use (4) more often, or have your partner block angle and you run to the line at the last instant.

The best defensive drill you can use would be for all four players to agree to some practice games with no blocking allowed. That's how we played the game as I grew up, and it taught me better defense. Concentrate on covering your half of the court as best you can, from dink to hard hit to deep shots. This drill will improve your anticipation better than any other.

Here's a good drill for picking up soft shots: have your partner stand with some balls, setting himself about five feet off the net. He's allowed to hit hard angle or a soft shot anywhere (deep line, deep angle, and sharp cut, among others). You start by standing in the angle. Then try to get every ball up. Meanwhile, the hitter runs under the net every time to set you, so you can practice scoring points. You should concentrate on taking a strong first step toward every shot, instead of quitting if you leaned the wrong way to start.

Another drill, this one for three players, is where one player sets himself while the other two block and play defense. Allow the blocker enough time to signal a call to the digger between plays. In this drill, the defense is doing well when it wins more than one out of every four rallies.

Serving

The only time you get to contact a volleyball without someone else having played it first is when you serve. So you've got to think of serving as an opportunity to seize a game and dictate how your opponents play, rather than just idly putting the ball over the net and praying for help from the volleyball gods.

Serving on the beach differs from indoors not in technique but in tactics. With the heavier ball, the wind, and only two players on the other side of the net, most players on the Pro Tour use the jump-serve. Just as teams decided in the early 1980s to play more aggressively by blocking every time, teams now jump-serve almost every time, against the wind and even with it.

For beginners, the first serve you should master is the floater that I described in the serving chapter. Face your target, use a low toss, contact the ball with the heel of your hand and your arm straight, just as you would indoors. You can hit the serve harder outdoors with the heavier ball (especially into the wind). The faster it travels the more it will dance around in the wind, and the more it dances the more trouble the other passer will have controlling it. A faster serve also gives the opposition less time to react. To make the ball travel faster, use your legs by stepping through, but also serve the ball with a very flat, low trajectory. That is, make it clear the net by a few inches, a foot or two at the most.

I prefer to jump-serve for a couple of reasons: First, the server puts the other team on the defensive. Passers know that every serve has the potential to be an ace. And second, some of those serves *will* be aces, because it's impossible for two players to cover the whole court. Two or three aces a game means you only have to earn twelve points to the opponents' fifteen.

The most important part of the jump-serve is the toss. Some servers use their left hand, others their right, and others use two hands. Some like their toss to have topspin (forward rotation), others want no spin; experiment with different tosses to see which works best for you. And just as with the floater, moving forward to meet the ball gives you more power so toss the ball out in front, and run forward to meet it.

As I discussed in the serving chapter, the jump-serve is really just a spike from the endline, which means that you have to contact the ball above or even behind your head so that it will go up (to cross the net) before it goes down. I use my right hand and I toss the ball up, with topspin, four to six feet in front of me and ten to twelve feet high (I like to keep the toss lower on the beach so the wind won't blow it around as much). Then just take your normal spike approach, be it three-step or four, and let loose.

If you decide to go for aces by serving harder, it's much better to err long than short into the net. Many times defensive players won't be able to judge whether the serve is inbounds or not, because the ball is dropping steeply. As a result, they might play some serves that would otherwise have gone out. But if the serve hits the net, or worse still, hits your partner in the back of the head, the opponents don't have to decide whether the ball is in or out—they get to laugh at you instead.

The third alternative you have on the beach is the skyball, especially if it's windy or the sun is straight overhead. Looking directly into the sun to pass can be excruciating. You hit this serve by crouching down, and then straightening your legs or even leaping up while sending an underhand serve high into the air. Some players like to serve it with spin, but if you can serve it with no spin, so it will move like a floater as it descends, it's much more effective.

One footnote: now that we play with the rally clock, a skyball can be an effective way of killing the last few seconds of a game. I guess I should have developed a good one for that purpose, but my partner and I like to keep playing aggressively, even through the end of a game, so I have a pathetic skyball.

Before talking strategy, I want to emphasize how important it is to have a specific goal in mind before every serve. Even if you don't make the serve do what you wanted it to, having a purpose will cut down your errors and make you a more accurate server. And no matter what type of serve you use, make the passers move to play the ball by serving where they aren't. Everyone can pass well when the ball falls right into their lap, so make the other team work to play the ball.

If you win the toss, elect to take the side facing into the wind. Serving and hitting into it can be a huge advantage, because the wind pushes the ball inbounds allowing you to serve with more power. If there's no wind, take the serve and make the other team decide which side is best.

Study your opponents. Maybe you'll find one of them has trouble passing balls served chest-high. In that case, you'd serve flat and deep. Or maybe he has trouble hitting after a short approach—so serve him short. Maybe one team lets serves drop between them out of indecision—serve into the seam and make them decide every time.

Another tactic teams use is to serve one player every ball to wear him out, especially if he's smaller and has to work harder to jump and hit each time. As he fatigues, he may make more errors or just crack mentally under the pressure of having to receive every serve.

To practice and improve your serves, use the same drills I described in the serving chapter: stretch some elastic across the net to practice lower-trajectory serves; mark the sidelines, corners, and seams and see how many times you can serve into those optimum areas; serve into the marked areas in succession, for instance, short line, deep line, deep middle, deep angle, short angle; and you can even play one-on-one with a partner where each of you plays the left or right half of the court, and you try to see who can ace whom more out of ten or twenty tries.

Team Offense

The key to winning the beach game is consistent team offense. Beach volleyball is a very simple game: pass, set, and hit. There are no secrets of gimmicks—it's just plain hard work. At top levels, teams perform the routine of pass, set, and hit so well, so consistently, it can be boring to watch. That monotonous perfection was the hallmark of two of the most successful careers in history: those of Ron von Hagen and Sinjin Smith.

Consistency also means never making mistakes, never letting the other team up for air. Almost all of it is mental: thinking before every play, "I *will* pass this ball well and I *will* put it away, or at worst keep it in play." If you sideout *every* time, you will eventually win, even if you only earn points on your opponents' mistakes. Don't lose patience with crawling toward the finish rather than sprinting. Follow von Hagen's best advice: "Never give up two points in a row." That should slow things down enough to win most games.

Consistent offense starts with good team passing. There are two important things to keep in mind while you and your partner try to pass serve. The first is where you two stand on the court (your starting locations) and the second is how well you two communicate, both before the play starts and as the play develops.

Obviously, two players dividing one court leaves one half of the court for each of you to cover, but it's not exactly half. Since it takes more time for the ball to travel crosscourt then down the line (because the crosscourt ball has to travel farther), the passer on the *angle* should generally try to take *more* of the middle area. For instance, if the server is standing down your line, your partner should take more of the middle. If, on the other hand, the server stands diagonally away from you, *you* need to take more middle. I actually shift over to my right a foot or two in an effort to cover more of that middle.

The only exception to this rule is when your partner is tired, hurt, cramping, or just playing poorly—then you should take all of the middle no matter where the serve is coming from. Other than these few exceptions, don't try to take all of the middle because, against a good jump-server it's physically impossible to cover that much of the court.

The second thing you need to do is communicate before the serve to reinforce this middle coverage concept: something simple like, "I've got the middle," works great. If you've played with your partner long enough, you won't need to say this, because you both will be thinking about it before every serve.

As the serve comes over the net, you should still be talking to each other. If it's in the middle, one of you should call for it, and the other should confirm that call: "I got it," "Yes." Or: "You got it," "Mine." These quick calls will help stop these infamous "husband and wife" serves from falling between you. If you see the ball is going to your partner, give him help with a "good" or "out" or "short" or "deep" call to let him know if the serve is in, and get him moving in the right direction.

Here are some ways you can adjust if things aren't going so well on offense. Maybe your partner is having trouble passing or siding out. You could move over a step to make it harder for the other team to serve him. If you or your partner are struggling with short serves, cheat up toward the net a step. Or take a step back if your opponents keep serving deep.

If a jump-server gets hot and hits a few bullets, take a time-out to cool him off. Or if he keeps hitting the jump-serve to the same part of the court, *both* of you should lean that way, or, to adjust even more, both of you should move a foot or two toward that area. If the serve keeps going to one sideline, both of you take a step that way. If it's going middle, you can both squeeze in. Another passing tactic players use is to start on one spot on the court, wait for the server to toss the ball up, and then move to cover more of a different area. That way you can show the server an open middle and take it away once it's too late for him to change.

How do you put the ball away every time with a big blocker up? The best way is to make sure the setter does a lot of the work. After every set, he should immediately tell the hitter whether a blocker is there or not. If there's no block, he should say something like, "Nobody up, hit away!" If there *is* a block up, the setter should then look and see where the digger is, and tell the hitter. For example, the setter might say, "He's up, cut it, cut it," if there is a blocker up and a digger standing down the line.

With that kind of help, the hitter doesn't go cross-eyed trying to see both the ball and the digger simultaneously. All he has to do is listen to the call and hit it to that spot. It helps the hitter if you say it twice ("Cut, cut," or "Line, line"), so that he can get the message from his ears to his hitting arm in midair. Just make sure the call is correct. Sometimes the digger will fake around in the backcourt two or three times before making a move. In that case, the setter has to wait longer to give the correct call.

To practice following the setter's call, hit sets of ten or twenty balls while the setter calls "angle," "line," or "nobody" at the last second. Try to make the right shot every time. To make things more realistic, the setter can mix in, "line, no, angle," to simulate a digger faking in the backcourt, or occasionally say nothing, in which case you have to make a good shot on your own.

Team Defense

What about team defense? If you follow beach volleyball, I'm sure you've seen what has become the norm on the Pro Tour: teams serving tough jump-serves, with a good blocker and a mobile defensive player working together to score points and force mistakes.

With a fast, high-pressure pace like this, verbal communication and a plan are the keys to building a tough defense. For example, before you serve you could say to your partner, "Okay, I'm going to jump-serve hard down the line to the short guy. You stand so you look like you're going to block line, and jump in to block his angle at the last minute; I'll fake digging the angle and run late to get the soft line shot."

Adjust your strategy to particular players. First, observe players in other matches and note what their favorite shots are. For instance, if the player is short, he may prefer to use his soft shots most of the time instead of hitting hard. When you play against him, mix in some fake block plays. The blocker can fake block and run to get the cut shot on the angle, or fake and run straight back to pick up the looping line shot. In either scenario, the digger would cover the opposite spot.

Conditioning and Training

As I mentioned before, a common tactic is to constantly serve the same player in an attempt to tire him out, especially if he's smaller and has to work harder to jump and hit each time. If all teams in a tournament use this tactic, near the end the player should be so tired that he will either start making errors on routine plays, or just cramp up, making for an even easier victory.

This strategy of trying to exploit a lack of conditioning, is one you not only may employ but will have employed against you as well. And even if other teams don't pick on you, with two players instead of six, theoretically you'll need three times the stamina plus the fact that the beach game demands more of your body because tournaments force you to play up to six or seven hours in one day, two or three days in a row.

As you can see, you can't play sideout volleyball if you lack endurance. Superb conditioning lets you sideout, and sideout, and sideout. The best way to assure great conditioning is to play more games during the week than you ever would during a tournament; but few people have the time, or three friends who have the time, for playing that many games. I like to practice about two and a half to three hours, two to three days a week during the season, since I'm competing every Saturday and Sunday. I also lift weights two days and stretch four to five days per week during the season.

Refer to the chapter on strength and conditioning to set up your own program. Just make it more specific to beach volleyball. For example, try to perform your jump training routine on soft sand. Or play with the weight belt on.

During long game you also need to be mentally solid to outlast the other team. Mental toughness isn't easy to define. One way to think of it is your mind's ability to push your body through new stress. When you are dead tired near the end of a day's games, practice making yourself play better than if you were fresh. Then push your body through some sprints. Then make yourself hit fifty balls and sprint after each one. *Then* you're mentally tough: your mind will have complete control over your body. From that point you just have to remember to tell your body what to do every play. Your body needs a lot of reminding, like being told to pass or set that next ball perfectly. And the next ball, and the next . . .

More Drills

For simplicity, I'll start this section with drills that you can do by yourself, or with just one other player. These drills are a good way to hone your ball control skills; the better ball control you have, the better player you'll be. Start by getting together as many balls as you can. The more you have, the longer you can drill without shagging.

1. Standing shots: Put hula hoops, circles of string, or a few big shirts down in three corners of the court: the sharp angle, deep line, and deep angle. Stand two or three feet off the net, throw the ball up, and (without jumping) wrist ten soft shots toward each of the three targets, aiming at the middle of each target so that, in case you err a bit, the ball will remain inbounds. A good goal is hitting the target five out of ten times on the angle and three or four of ten to the two deep areas. Remember to use the same hitting motion until the instant before contact, when your wrist breaks and you direct the ball to each particular area. If your opponents normally don't block, you can keep your shots low; otherwise, play them higher to practice hitting over the blocker.

2. Standing, off the net: Repeat the first drill but stand about ten feet off the net, as if you were hitting a bad set. Expect to hit the target less often, since your shots have to travel farther. The angle shot is most difficult here, but if you can still hit the target, you've developed a great cut shot.

3. Set to yourself: Repeat drill *1.* while throwing the ball up higher (or have a partner set you, if possible) and jumping to hit.

4. Set to yourself, off the net: Repeat drill *2.* while throwing the ball up higher (or have a partner set you) and jumping to hit.

5. Off-side drills: Repeat drills *1. to 4.*, this time on your weaker side. If you normally play on the left, as I do, repeat the drills from the right. My right-side cut stinks, so I'm trying to improve it for when I need to score points after digging on the right side behind my partner's block.

6. Partner calling shots: Repeat drills *1. to 4.*, having a partner call a shot at the last second: "Cut" or "Line" (or words to that effect). Try to listen and react, making the correct shot. You can even have your partner make the wrong call, then change it ("Deep, no, angle") to make it really difficult.

7. Called shots, off-side: Repeat drill on *6.* your weak side.

8. Bump setting: Lay down your target close to the net where your partner's ideal set should go. Toss up high, spinning balls (throw them to yourself or have a partner do it) that mimic digs off hard-driven spikes, bump-setting them to the target. Perform this drill from all areas including behind the endline and very close to the net. Bad sets are the number one reason why digs aren't converted into points, so this is important.

9. Hand setting: Repeat drill *8.* but set with your hands.

10. Off-side setting: Repeat drills *8.* and *9.* from your weaker side to practice for scramble plays.

For two players, a good drill is the one I described above in the beach defense section where the digger has to get up hard hits on one side of the court and soft shots that can go anywhere on the court from a hitter who sets himself from off the net.

If only three people happen to show up, hit ten or twenty balls (from a setter) against a blocker. Or compete using the drill I mentioned above in the beach blocking section: hitter vs.

blocker. Or have one player set himself against a team (blocker and digger) and see how many balls the team can dig and convert out of twenty balls (five or more scored is good).

If you can get four players together to play some games, ask your opponents to play at your weaknesses. The more time you spend on deficiencies, the more consistent your game becomes. You want to set better? Have your partner cover more of the court while you try to set every pass with your hands. So what if you throw a few? So what if you throw a lot? That's why they call it a "practice" game. Even take digs with your hands. Sometimes when I'm practicing, we'll loosen the setting calls to encourage ourselves to use our hands.

Use practice games to set quotas for yourself as well. For example, allow yourself two throws, three bad passes, and two out hits. Oops, there's 7 points already. See how quickly they add up? Stay within your quota, and next time make it more stringent. Slowly you can force yourself toward playing mistake-free sideout volleyball.

We do the "sideout drill" almost every workout. It helps you concentrate on your siding out, blocking, or serving and defense, depending on where you are in the drill. Just have one player on one team serve thirty straight balls (missed serves count as half a point for the sideout team) and play defense, while his partner blocks against the other team that tries to sideout every play. A good goal for the sideout team is to win the game 24 to 6, because any time you can limit the opposition to scoring only one point out of every four tries, you should win. When you're serving, this drill is also good for your conditioning. Jump-serving and playing defense thirty times in a row can get you winded. Try to rest as little as possible between plays—the pace should be fast. After a game of 30 points is done, the teams should switch sides, repeat, switch sides again, repeat, and switch once more and repeat so that every player served once, blocked once, and sided out twice. Or, if you're not concerned about staying together with a particular partner, you all can just rotate through so you serve, block, sideout on the left, and sideout on the right. To make it most challenging for the sideout team, give the serving team the good side so it can serve into the wind.

We also use a variation of the sideout drill, in which the two teams actually compete. The serving team keeps serving and trying to score a total of 20 points while the sideout team has to sideout three times in a row to earn 1 big point. It has to score 6 of those big points before the serving team reaches 20.

Here's a good game to use instead of playing regular games to 15 all the time. It's called a "wash" game. Teams take turns serving, and the only way a team can earn a point is if it wins both the rally when it served and the sideout when the other team served. If the teams split those plays, it's a "wash" and the team that received first the previous time serves first the next. This kind of game lasts longer than a regular one, so we often play to 11 points instead of 15. The reason I like a wash is that you also have to sideout well if you want to score points, just like you have to sideout well if you expect to win in regular competition. It's also great training for anyone who plays with a rally clock, to get used to siding out as the clock expires to win a big game.

If you can get eight players together, here's a great conditioning drill which we call "eight-man frenzy": it's a king-of-the-mountain theme where the object is for your team to work its way over to the side of the net where you receive serves and stay there for as many plays as you can, earning as many sideouts as you can until you give up a point. Then you're booted and you have to start all over. One team (team #1) starts siding out, a second team (team #2) lines up across the net to block and dig (to prevent the sideout), a third team (team #3) waits behind team #2's endline with one player ready to serve, and the fourth team (team #4) stands behind the same endline, also with one player holding a ball ready to serve.

Team #3 serves the ball, and any of four things can happen: (1) if team #3 makes a service error, that team steps to the back of the line, team #4 serves the next ball, team #2 stays to block and dig, and team #1 stays siding out and gets one point (for the sideout on the service error); (2) if the serve goes in and team #1 sides out, team #1 gets a point. Team #2 failed to stop them and so steps to the back of the line. Team #3 steps into the court to replace them while team #4 serves the next ball; (3) if the serve goes in an team #1 doesn't sideout, team #1 runs to the back of the line at the far endline. Team #2 runs under the net to get ready to sideout while team #3 steps into the court to block and dig, and team #4 serves the next ball with nobody having earned any points; (4) Lastly, if team #3 serves an ace, it earns a point and gets to leapfrog over to the sideout court. Team #1 goes to the back of the line, while team #2 stays blocking and digging and team #4 steps up to serve.

It sounds a lot more complicated than it really is. The conditioning element comes from these two tricks: (1) The net serve can come *as soon as* the last play ended, so the next team always has to be ready to serve, and all players have to be ready to sprint to their next position; (2) The drill goes on for ten minutes, non-stop, or until someone keels over. Whoever accumulates the most sideouts (each worth one point) plus aces, wins. A couple of these games and you'll feel like you've gotten a two-hour workout because of the quick serving.

A variation that we use most often is to play with this rule: when you finally work your way over to the sideout court, if you don't earn a sideout on the first play, your team *loses* a point and goes back to the end of the line. That can be the killer, because often you and your teammate are sprinting under the net at full speed and still can't get there in time to play the serve that came over and hit the back line. Also, it becomes almost a disadvantage to serve an ace, because your team has to sprint from the service line all the way to the other court, all while the next team serves.

Conclusion

I really think you should spend some time developing your beach skills. First, it'll force you to become a better all-around player. You'll learn better ball control and it will force you into better condition. With the continual rise in popularity of beach volleyball both domestically and abroad, there will be more opportunities and more tournaments in which to test your skills, including a chance to compete in the Olympics representing your country. And lastly, it's fun. So have at it.

14

QUESTIONS AND ANSWERS

1. *Karch, regarding the two-passer scheme: Do you think that it is the ideal system for serve reception? What are its strong and weak points?*

I think that the two-passer system plays a major role in the long-developing trend toward more specialization in volleyball. Our USA team had players who specialized in hitting from the backrow, players who specialized in hitting quicksets, players who specialized in setting, even players who specialized in serving and backrow defense. So, for our team, the two-passer system was ideal.

I talked about the advantages of the two-passer system in Chapter 8: passing is easier when handled by two players rather than by five, because two need less communication, can assign areas of responsibility on the court more precisely, and have fewer bodies (obstacles) in their way. The two passers concentrate better because they are involved in every play, and even start out in the same position most of the time; they exempt other players from passing so that they can concentrate on their own strengths; and using only the team's two best passers guarantees a higher percentage of perfect passes.

This may not necessarily be the best system for all teams, though. For example, a team with four very good passers doesn't have to worry about hiding weak passers, so it can afford to use all four players in the passing scheme. If I were coach, I would do just that. If a team did not want to use a backrow attack, then it could ignore the need to free up a hitter back there and use another passer instead.

On the other hand, I don't see teams switching to fewer than two passers. There aren't any athletes capable of covering the whole court by themselves. In the future, maybe, but not now.

So what is a coach to do? Each team is unique and needs its own special system to help it reach its potential. Part of the art of coaching is deciding how to blend the talent you have together into the best team. If a team has three great passers, then use them. If it has only two, then use them and no more.

2. *Karch, what in your team's long-term plan helped you win the Triple Crown? Were there any special strategies for beating the Soviets?*

There were three main keys to our success—and they all happened in 1981. First, we brought the training center from Dayton, Ohio, out west to San Diego, California. Many new players joined the team, better athletes than we had previously, mainly because the new training center was closer to their homes. Second, we put a great coach in charge of the program. Doug Beal analyzed the talent he had available and, over a three-year period, refined our system. This system became the nucleus of our Olympic team. We used essentially the same system from 1984 to 1988—although with different players. During those years the American system depended on two good hitter/passers, a strong setter, a great outside/backrow hitter opposite the setter, and two strong middle blocker/quick-hitters.

We set goals for ourselves every year. For instance, in 1982 we wanted to finish in the top five at the World Championships. We failed dismally. But after three or four years of very hard training, with some disasters and some successes under our belt, we became a much better team, and we started to surpass more and more of our goals. We never achieved all of them. We always set our goals a little too high to be able to succeed at every one. The most crucial thing is to succeed at your most important goal. In 1986 we set out, as our two highest goals, to win the World

Championship and then to win the Goodwill Games. We failed at the second-highest priority, but we didn't mind because we succeeded at our top priority goal—the World Championship.

Again, what helped us become so good? Great athletes, a great coach, hard training, and setting high standards for ourselves were major ingredients in our recipe for greatness.

As to whether we developed any special strategy for the Soviets —we actually did that for every team we played. We analyzed, using video, scouting reports, and computers, each of our opponents rotation by rotation, player by player, to decide how to defend and block that team. For example, the Soviets used many playsets, so we tried to pull more blockers into the middle of the court to neutralize their offense. We couldn't afford to fasten our sights solely on the Soviets, though, since our goal was to be better than *every* team. Because we all have to play so many different teams, I think it's important to play your own game the best you can and let everything fall into place. Sometimes we didn't play as well when we were thinking too much about the other team, or looking past that team and thinking too much about the next team we had to face, and not just thinking about playing our own game.

3. *If you could organize the perfect team, what kind of character would each of the six players possess, and how would these characters mesh to form the team?*

First of all, I'd take six kids who I knew were going to grow taller than six feet, five inches (preferably around six feet, eight inches), and that were going to be able to jump at least 40 inches, and start them playing volleyball at age five or six. As they grew up I'd teach them to pass and play defense like Aldis Berzins. I'd teach three of them to hit like Steve Timmons, another two to hit like Pat Powers, and the sixth player to set like Stan Gosciniak (the great Polish setter of the mid-seventies).

I'd teach them all to block like Raymond Vilde or Craig Buck. And, finally, I'd teach all six of them to serve like Eric Sato. Then I'd have the greatest team the history of this game has ever seen or ever will see. Luckily, no one country can have all the best players, so we all can go to tournaments knowing that anything can happen and any team can win.

As to character, I think the setter should have the coolest head, because he's the one who has to do the most thinking out on the court. Everyone else can just be themselves—as long as they can all get along to a reasonable degree. Even an occasional fight isn't a big problem, as long as the players apologize right away, and use the emotion to their advantage.

4. *Please select the six best players in the world, and give us your reasons.*

This isn't a fair question because you're asking me to rate my peers. I don't want to hurt the feelings of any of my ex-teammates or those of any other players by leaving them off the list. It's also unfair because different systems need different types of players. Magic Johnson, for example, was a great basketball player for the Lakers, but he might not have been as good playing on a different team—like the Boston Celtics. It's also unfair because there are so many good players all around the world.

The last and best reason for not naming the best six is that, as players or coaches, we should learn to think about how best to use the players we have on our teams—not the ones we wish we had. Granted, it's good for players to have role models. However, a top-notch player like Craig Buck is not necessarily a good role model for little kids, because a player has to be six feet, eight inches tall just to begin emulating Craig. You have to think in terms of developing a system that gets the most out of the players you have.

One last note: In Question 4 I identified the key skills of some of the best players in the world. Use these skills, rather than the players themselves, as role models.

5. *Would you tell us how a player like yourself, of "medium" size, is able to hit past blockers who are much larger than you? How do you practice this?*

One thing that helps me very much is having a good jump. Anyone can improve their jump by doing the exercises I talked about in the "Strength and Conditioning" chapter. Another thing that helped me a lot was our offense: we had so many good hitters drawing the attention of opposing blockers that I was often left in one-on-one hitting situations, which are easy for any hitter to put away.

The rest of the time, I depend on trying to reach very high, extending my arm as much as possible when I'm hitting the ball. Hitting low is one of the best ways I know to guarantee that the ball will be blocked back into your face. Hitting high and deep is safer—even if the blockers touch the ball, they won't block it down to the floor very often. Usually it will bounce back over your head out of bounds, or over the blockers' heads and out of bounds, or at least be left in play.

As I mentioned earlier, a good way to practice hitting high and deep is to hit at chairs set deep in the court, or else to hit at the last six feet of the court.

It also helps to be able to see where the blockers are with your peripheral vision. You can practice this by hitting against one blocker who makes radical moves one way or the other, either jumping way into the angle or way out to the line. You, as the hitter, have to hit in the opposite direction. Don't ever look directly at the blocker. Instead, use your peripheral vision while keeping your eyes on the ball. As you get better, you'll start seeing holes to hit through, or blockers' hands to hit the ball off of and out of bounds.

Seeing the block and reaching high are equally important— master these two keys and you will be an unstoppable hitter.

6. *What influence does beach volleyball have on indoor volleyball? Can playing on the beach be useful training for indoor volleyball?*

I like the beach game because it teaches you how to play every phase of the game well. For our USA team this was important, because we didn't have that many all-around players, and we wanted the whole team to play better defense. That's why our coach, Marv Dunphy, encouraged all of us to get out on the beach, on our own, and play as much as possible. But we did not have any organized team training on the beach. Beach volleyball can be useful training, but it's more important for bigger players who can't pass or play defense than it is for players who have already developed good ball control skills.

I now train exclusively on the beach. It keeps me in good shape and increases my jumping ability without hurting my knees or my back. That way I also increase my longevity. So if you want to get in better condition and increase your jump without risking injuries, the beach is a good answer. The harder our team trained indoors, the more injuries we had. So use the beach to stay healthy and strong.

7. *Do you have any advice on how to organize a team, and how to schedule training and games over the course of the year?*

It was easier for me to play hard the whole year when we

went through training cycles. We would usually start slowly in the early part of the year, go on a couple of tours, train harder and harder, and then play in a tournament in the middle of the year. Then we'd take a few weeks off and start over, running through a couple more cycles until we finished for the year. Then we would take a month of vacation. It's destructive to players' bodies and minds to ask them to be at their best all year long. Give your team some easy opponents early on and take some time off, so that it can come back to play better as the year goes on and be at its best as your most important goals approach. If we had tried to be at our best for 12 straight months, we'd have gone insane with frustration—that's asking the impossible. Schedule your practices and games with the important tournaments in mind, and concentrate on peaking for those few tournaments.

Unfortunately, it's more difficult in some states and countries because you have both club seasons and interscholastic seasons—and different coaches have different priorities. Playing in both seasons forces players to double the time that they have to be at their best—which isn't always possible. I would encourage coaches to work together to decide what their most important goals are for each year, and set their training schedules accordingly.

8. *How do you choose a partner on the beach? What do you look for? Is physical or mental strength more important?*

When I first partnered with Sinjin Smith in 1979, I thought we would complement each other well: we both played very consistent, mistake-free volleyball; he had won tournaments before, so he was proven (although I wasn't—so he took more of a chance playing with me); he played the right side well, while I played the left; and neither of us had any glaring weaknesses or strengths, so that there was no obvious choice as to whom to serve at, no major flaw to exploit.

I guess I look for consistency, a proven ability to win, someone who can play the right side well, and team balance.

I think it helps to be strong both mentally *and* physically. Each player has to believe that he will make the big play, and keep making the small ones, so that his team is capable of lasting a whole tournament. The top players rarely, if ever, tire in the late going.

9. *How do you feel about beach volleyball's first-ever inclusion in the Olympics in 1996; and what impact do you feel it will have on the sport in America?*

Any sport that's not already part of the Olympic program aspires to be included, even sports like golf, bowling, and chess. So overall, I think beach volleyball players and fans should consider it an honor that their sport is now a full-fledged medal sport for 1996. I am very disappointed, however, in the Olympic qualification process that the FIVB has mandated, because I believe that it is not a "fair and open" process as required by U.S. law in the Amateur Sports Act of 1978. In order to qualify for and participate in the Olympics, a team must earn a certain number of points. It sounds simple enough, but the problem is that a team can only earn points for Olympic qualification by participating in FIVB sanctioned events. The FIVB is a new tour, and so does not attract the kind of talent that the AVP tour does. Because of conflicting schedules, the top caliber teams on the AVP tour can't participate in nearly enough FIVB events. As a result, our country will not have its three best teams competing in the 1996 Atlanta Olympics, and fans around the world will not be exposed to the highest level of beach volleyball available.

I also believe that the 1996 Olympics will have a strong, positive impact on beach volleyball, and on volleyball in general, because of the exposure that beach volleyball should receive during the five or six days of competition. Beach volleyball has never shared the stage as part of the world's largest multisport event, and occupying a part of that stage will lend the sport more credibility in the eyes of the media (hopefully leading to more press coverage of all types of volleyball in the future) and in the eyes of sports fans who follow only pro football, baseball, or basketball. My only worry is that the beach and indoor volleyball competitions might compete with each other for airtime. But, ultimately, the sport should double its exposure at the Olympics, and that can only augur well for the next four years.

10. *What is a "backslide" set? Several times I have seen teams run a play where the setter sets the ball to the weak side out and high. The ball is then hit by the middle hitter who slides out, jumping off of one foot. Is that a "backslide?"*

First, by "weak side" I assume you mean the right side of the court. We never referred to it as the "weak side." If anything, our hitters were even stronger on that side. Look at Steve Timmons hitting from the right side out of the backrow—nothing weak about that.

Each team probably has its own names for its own sets, and there's no harm in that at all. When different teams try to figure out what to call each other's sets, though, a terminology like the one explained in Chapters 7 and 8 comes in handy. For the USA team, a backslide was a quickset, about an 81, where the quick-hitter approached from middle front and jumped close to the setter, then drifted past him in the air, contacting the set about three feet *behind* the setter. So your version of the backslide is not what ours was.

A frontslide was just the opposite—the quick-hitter approached from the right front and slid past the setter for a 41 or 51, depending upon where the setter stood. The purpose of both these sets was to force the opposing middle blocker to move in one direction or another. If the middle blocker didn't follow the quick-hitter, we set him. If the middle blocker did follow, then something else would open up.

11. *I've heard about various "muscle-memory" programs for sports. One hour of concentrated muscle-memory training does as much as 10 hours of hard, consistent physical practice, say some of the program's authors. Do you believe this, or is this just a sales job?*

I honestly think that muscle-memory training may have its place as a supplement in a volleyball player's training regimen. But this program seems all too typical of our society: we're always looking for the magic pill to help us lose weight instead of eating right and exercising; we're always looking for the easy, immediate, quick-fix solution or gratification instead of sacrifice, hard work, and long-term solutions. Anyone who tells you that they can be as good with 1 hour of thinking as they could be with 10 hours of hard work can't be a winner except in the Lazy Man's Hall of Fame. "No deposit, no return," as I once heard John Naber, the American swimming star, say. But if you perform the 1 hour of muscle-memory training in addition to the 10 hours of hard work—yes, you might become better. The more you put in, the more you'll get out.

EPILOGUE

I have, as I'm sure many of you do, a vision of what volleyball will become in the future. I see our sport becoming more exciting, becoming more popular (especially here in the US), and growing into one of the two largest participatory sports in the world (if it isn't already).

What are some of my goals? I'd like to see much more live radio and television coverage of volleyball throughout the world. I'd like to see a number of different forms of volleyball become popular: mixed (men and women together) volleyball, indoor and beach volleyball, junior and senior championships, and outdoor tours—worldwide—for both men and women. We could even have so-called alumni matches where just for the fun of it we get players from different eras together to play exhibition matches.

My vision of the game is beginning to approach reality. Television is starting to show more live volleyball. Indoor volleyball, both men's and women's, received tremendous exposure during the 1984 and 1988 Olympics. Beach volleyball is very popular in the US and in countries like Brazil, Italy, Japan, and Australia.

Dr. Ruben Acosta, president of the FIVB (Fédération Internationale de Volleyball), came to Los Angeles in December 1986 to address some of the challenges still ahead. He realized that we have to work harder here in the US to make sure that volleyball attracts the attention it deserves. The American market is crucial to our success, because without conquering that market, volleyball will never be considered a legitimate sport.

Few people here really know what kind of skill it takes to master the game. We have almost 25 million recreational players here, but the majority play a rudimentary game, alien to high-level volleyball, in which any number of people just bat the ball back and forth across the net instead of actually using all three legal contacts and playing as a team. Many recreational players don't even know what a pass or a set is. I think that if we can show those recreational players just how much expertise is required, they will be so impressed that we'll have won over millions rather than thousands of avid fans. The only way to teach them the difference is to expose them en masse to what real volleyball is all about. And the medium for this exposure has to be television.

The FIVB proposed an attack on many fronts. It wanted to develop beach volleyball, and change indoor volleyball to package it more efficiently for television. It even took a stand on political issues. For example, the FIVB stated that if any country boycotts the Olympics, that country's volleyball federation will be expelled and will no longer be allowed to participate in organized competition. That was the first time an individual sports-governing body had taken a political stand—just one of a number of steps that the FIVB is taking to ensure that volleyball will be on the leading edge of amateur sports in the years to come.

I would like to think that by offering several types of volleyball to the American public, we have a better chance of capturing its attention. Each person will have his or her own preferences. We can offer them beach volleyball, national-team volleyball, college volleyball, high school and junior volleyball— and each of those comes in both male and female forms. These packages offer alternatives to people who don't know much about volleyball. That's why the FIVB plans to get more involved. The crossover of players from the beach to indoors and back can help increase the total audience that volleyball reaches.

The AVP (Association of Volleyball Professionals) has had an even larger impact on the beach game. From 1977, the year of the first professional tournament, until 1995, when the tour had a total purse of nearly 4.5 million dollars, the AVP has been the driving force in the explosion of its popularity. Tour events now take place nationwide, from Miami to New York, from New Orleans to Seattle, from Chicago to Honolulu, and from Milwaukee to Dallas.

Many people feel that for volleyball to break through to a higher level of popularity, the game itself will have to be modified. As it stands, an international match can last anywhere from 45 minutes to 4 hours. This usually precludes a live show, because broadcasters can only program finite time slots for each event. But live broadcasts attract the most attention and publicity. If the game is shown weeks later, it's old news and the audience will have dwindled.

How can the game lengths be made more consistent? The best way seems to be to change the scoring rules. For beach volleyball, I think the answer is the rally clock we use on the Lite/AVP Tour.

For indoor volleyball I think there is still too much variation in the length of a match. A good solution would be to play a quick-score system (points are awarded on each play, no matter which team serves) but play best-of-three matches rather than best-of-five. The fewer the sets played, the more predictable the match length becomes. The first two sets could be much longer, so that even if the match goes two straight games, it will last at least one and a half hours. Then the third game could be a very short sudden-death game so that the total match length will not go much over two hours. I also believe that once one team scores a set number of points during the course of action, the quick-score system should be revoked (for both teams), and scoring returned to the style that we play with now, where points are scored only on a serve. (Of course, some might argue that if we have to change back, we are admitting that the old system is better, so why change in the first place?)

Several of these experiments have been tested in Team Cup volleyball, the men's pro indoor league held for years at the Forum in Los Angeles. Both the two-out-of-three and quick-scoring formats worked very well. For example, the teams played the first two games quick-score to 27 points, and then finished the game (scoring only on serve) to 30 points. If the match went to a third game, teams played a tiebreaker quick-score to 10 points, and then needed to earn only 1 more point (again, on serve) to finish the game to 11. It worked very well because each match lasted between one and a quarter and one and a half hours. When a match went to a third game, it was very exciting—the game was short and pressure-packed like a tiebreaker in tennis.

There is another problem to address. In men's volleyball the disparity between offense and defense has grown steadily in the last ten years. More often than not, the rallies are short: pass, set, and *boom*, the ball is terminated. In women's volleyball, on the other hand, the rallies are sometimes too long. So how do we achieve a happy medium? Somehow the men's defense has to be given some additional advantage.

You would think that longer rallies (because of a stronger defense) would lead to longer games, but the FIVB has found that the opposite is true. Longer rallies mean that more point opportunities arise for the serving team, so the games are shorter. This could help package the game for television better.

Some of the ideas for balancing the offense and defense are: to move the 10-foot line backward to thwart the backcourt attack; to make backrow hitters land behind (instead of jump from behind) the 10-foot line—for the same effect; to raise the height of the net (although this would legislate smaller players out of the game); to allow both teams to position a seventh player out on the floor to assist on defense; to allow more substitution so that the better defensive players can come into the backrow more often; and to allow both teams to position an extra blocker at the net. How many of these are really feasible is up to the FIVB to decide.

As Doug Beal has noted, a problem will arise when the rules are changed for one effect (game duration) without also addressing the other change (balancing offense and defense). Now that the game duration has changed, any defensive change could knock out of whack whatever good the first change accomplished. It could nullify or amplify any of the good effects.

Until we decide upon the changes, if any, that we'll make to our game, I can't say what the future holds for volleyball strategy. If no changes are made, I'd say that the backrow attack will become an increasingly important part of every team's offense. Teams may go so far as to run quicksets to backrow hitters, and some teams already use five hitters in every rotation—with everyone except the setter hitting. That way teams can exert more and more pressure on the blockers and the defense and keep the advantage on their side of the net.

One thing I can say is that we should all try to have an open mind and be ready to embrace new ideas that might help the game reach a wider audience. When I was in Japan for the 1986 Japan Cup, we tried playing games to 12 points, with a 1-point margin required for victory. Predictably, teams that benefited from the change liked it, while those that suffered, disliked it. Some teams resisted the proposed change based solely on the threat it made to their perceived advantages. The Soviets, for instance, argued that the experiment was wrong because one mistake, by a referee or a player, could end the game. But hasn't this always been true? If your team is losing 14–11, one mistake could end the game for you.

We have to think of the future of our sport as a whole. Selfish interests have to be ignored. Players can't think about whether a rule change helps their own game or not—they have to think about whether the change is in the best interests of volleyball. We're lucky to have such an exciting sport to play, to watch, and to enjoy. Let's keep it that way for years to come.

GLOSSARY

ace: a point scored as the direct result of a serve, usually when the ball hits the floor untouched on the receiving team's side of the court.

antenna: the out-of-bounds marker at each end of the net, a thin pole extending three feet above the net.

backset: a type of set placed behind the setter's head, and directed to a spiker or hitter approaching from behind the setter.

block: a defensive play, made above the net by one or more players, which prevents the ball from crossing the net.

bump: generally, the receiving team's first contact with the serve. The receiver (or passer) directs the ball toward the setter to begin the offensive attack.

cut shot: a type of shot a hitter uses to misdirect the ball. The hitter contacts only a portion of the ball—away from its center—so that the ball comes away from his hand at a severe angle.

dig: a successful defensive recovery of a hard-driven spike or other attack.

dink: a soft shot delivered by the attacking team, gently placed around or above the opposing blockers.

double hit: when a player contacts the ball twice in a row; an illegal act, often called on the setter for mishandling a pass.

floater: to hit this type of serve the server contacts the ball near its center; this prevents it from spinning and creates a "floating" effect.

free ball: a call used by the defense to alert teammates to a lob or easy return on its way from the offense.

jump serve: to hit this type of serve the server contacts the ball after taking a running jump from behind the endline. This serve is hit with the velocity of a spike.

kill: an attack (usually a spike or dink) that the defense is unable to return.

kong block: a one-armed blocking style made popular on the pro beach circuit by Randy Stoklos.

overset: an errant set that crosses the net without being touched by another offensive player.

pass: the initial contact with the ball by a team within its own court, on receiving a serve or other attack from the opposing team. The passer tries to direct the ball to the setter who, in turn, tries to set one of his team's hitters.

quick scoring: a format for scoring in which points can be scored by either team on every serve.

rainbow: a soft shot over the blockers to the back line that has the arc of a rainbow.

serve: to start play by hitting the ball, starting from behind the endline, over the net to the receiving team.

serve reception: the first hit (a bump or pass) by the receiving team after the ball is served.

shank: a bad pass or dig that is untouchable by any of the other players on the court.

sideout: when the receiving team successfully prevents the serving team from scoring a point on the play started by the serve, the receiving team earns a sideout and the serve.

spike: to hit the ball downward with as much force as possible into your opponent's court.

stuff block: a dramatic block that leads directly to a point or sideout.

10-foot line: a dividing line located 10 feet back from and parallel to the net on both sides of the court. No backrow player may jump and contact the ball—either hitting or blocking—above the net from in front of the 10-foot line.

KARCH KIRALY'S VOLLEYBALL MILESTONES

1978 California State Championship (Santa Barbara High School) California Interscholastic Federation Prep Player of the year

1979 NCAA Championship (UCLA)
First-ever undefeated season by a collegiate team (UCLA)
NCAA All-American (UCLA)
First beach volleyball Open Victory
First beach volleyball World Championship (Sinjin Smith)
Six beach Open Victories total (Smith, Tim Hovland)

1980 NCAA All-American (UCLA)
Eight Open Victories (Smith, Peter Ehrman)

1981 NCAA Championship (UCLA), tournament Most Valuable Player
NCAA All-American (UCLA)
Joined U.S. National Team
Beach volleyball World Championship (Smith)
Six Open Victories (Smith)

1982   NCAA Championship (UCLA), tournament Most Valuable Player
NCAA All-American (UCLA)
Second-ever undefeated season by a collegiate team (UCLA)
One Open Victory (Smith)

1984   Olympic Gold Medal (Los Angeles), tournament Best Sportsman
Two Open Victories (Smith)

1985   World Cup Gold Medal (Japan), tournament Most Valuable Player Sullivan Award Finalist (for nation's outstanding amateur athlete)
Two Open Victories (Mike Dodd)

1986   World Championship Gold Medal (France)
Named World's Best Player (first time ever awarded) by FIVB
Sullivan Award Finalist
One Open Victory (Dodd)

1987   Pan American Games Gold Medal (Indianapolis)
Sullivan Award Finalist

1988   Olympic Gold Medal (Seoul, Korea), tournament Most Valuable Player
Named FIVB World's Best Player for second time
Sullivan Award Finalist
Beach FIVB World Championship (Pat Powers), Brazil
Two Open Victories (Powers, Ricci Luyties)

1989   Five Open Victories (Brent Frohoff, Steve Timmons)

1990   Seven Open Victories (Frohoff, Kent Steffes)
Voted AVP Most Valuable Player and Best Offensive Player

1991   Italian Professional League Championship (Il Messaggero club team)
Italian Cup Gold Medal (Il Messaggero)
World Club Championship Gold Medal (Il Messaggero)
Six Open Victories (Steffes)
Won Inaugural King of the Beach Tournament
AVP Best Offensive Player

1992   European Club Championship Gold Medal (Il Messaggero)
Sixteen Open Victories (Steffes), including record-tying thirteen consecutive wins

       Winner, U.S. Championships (Steffes)
       King of the Beach Champion
       AVP Most Valuable Player and Best Offensive Player

1993 Eighteen Open Victories (Steffes), new team season record
       Winner, U.S. Championships (Steffes)
       King of the Beach Champion
       AVP Most Valuable Player and Best Offensive Player

1994 Seventeen Open Victories (Steffes)
       Winner, U.S. Championships (Steffes)
       AVP Most Valuable Player and Best Offensive Player

1995 Thirteen Open Victories (Steffes, Scott Ayakatubby)
       AVP Most Valuable Player